Travel Alone & Love It

A Flight Attendant's Guide To Solo Travel

By
SHARON B. WINGLER

Evanston, Illinois

CHICAGO SPECTRUM PRESS
7210-D Adams Street
Willowbrook, Illinois 60521
630-654-1156

This book is intended as a *how-to* guide on solo travel. Every effort has been made to bring you the most accurate, current information possible. There may, nonetheless, be mistakes both typographical and in content. Medical findings are constantly being updated and some information in this book will become obsolete in time. Consult your own physician for your personal health concerns. Neither the author nor publisher shall have responsibity or liability to anyone for any injury, loss or damage alleged to be caused by the information in this book.

ISBN 1-886094-35-7

Library of Congress Number 96-84617

Printed in the U.S.A.

10 9 8 7 6 5 4 3

Photo Credits — Front Cover: "Santorini" and "Prague" by Sharon B. Wingler; "Beach on Andros, Bahamas" by COM-STOCK, INC. Back Cover: Author's photo by Patricia Valalik.

Book cover design by Ann E. Green of Green Design, Boulder, Colorado.

To my dear mom, Shirley Buynak, who thinks I'm perfect, and to Larry Hines, who knows I'm not but loves me anyway. And in memory of Mom's mom, Grace Taveggia, who was my soul mate and my soul teacher. You're with me always, Grandma.

ACKNOWLEDGMENTS

I am eternally grateful to Patricia Valalik who gave me my first journal, encouraging me to write, reflect and to seek joy. Thank you to Susan Bossert for sparking my initial idea to write this book. I wish to extend my great appreciation to all my friends at Delta for their encouragement and support, especially to Linda Duff, Alice Morin and Gail DiCicco. I owe thanks to Toni Turner for her unselfish advice.

My heartfelt gratitude goes to Lane Brady for her constant confidence in me and for sharing her wide network of friends.

This book would not be possible without the masterly editing of Joan Marie Moss. She has been most generous with her time, advice and considerable talent. Special thanks as well to Dorothy Kavka for her expertise and kindness in guiding me through the process of publication.

My undying thanks and love go to Larry for accepting my wanderlust and for never complaining about all the nights I spent computer wrestling instead of snuggling with him.

"We shall not cease from exploration, and the end of all our exploring will be to arrive where we started and know the place for the first time."

T. S. ELIOT

Contents

Introduction

This book is more than a practical "how-to" guide to help you in your solo travels. It is also my small (okay, very small) contribution to world peace through understanding.

In our lifetimes, we have seen the world become a closer, more reachable place. First, jet travel made it possible to travel within a day to almost any corner of the globe. Now, telecommunication brings us the world in an instant. Distant civilizations are now our neighbors. Globalization is the word of the day. We begin to realize that, not only are we all in the same boat, but the boat seems smaller than it used to be. A tree chopped down in Brazil affects the air in Brussels. Economies are interdependent. Understanding one another seems more and more important. Yet newsprint, pictures, live satellite images and sound bites do not give us the whole story. We humans are much more than our politics, crimes, wars and natural disasters. We are about family, friends, faith, values, sports, food, art, music, hobbies and habits.

Travel gives us first hand knowledge of a place and its people. Traveling alone gives us the greatest opportunity to meet and interact with people, one-on-one. Through meeting and interacting with people, we come to understand them and, in understanding, we will someday find peace. I want to inspire you to travel alone, not only for the sheer joy of it, but to help build bridges over the gaps in our knowledge of each other. I want to inspire you to engage and connect with the people you meet. Let them see the human side of your country. You, too, are more than your politics, crime, wars and natural disasters. Let our travels lead us to knowledge, understanding and peace.

By the time you read this, I will have logged over twenty-six years as a flight attendant for Delta Air Lines. My job has taken me all over the country; my vacations have taken me all over the world. A real love of travel has been a part of me for as long as I can remember, though I did not even take my first flight until the age of eighteen.

It was not my original intention to travel alone. I had plenty of friends to travel with in the early years of my career, then a spouse. My husband and I took two big trips together each of the twelve years we were married.

I was divorced at age thirty-five and, among other things, without a travel partner for the first time in my life. I still had plenty of friends, but they were not as footloose and ready to go at thirty-five as they'd been at twenty. For me, the choice was now to stay home or go alone. The thought of going alone scared me, but to stay at home was simply unthinkable. I made up my mind to be brave and at least give solo travel a try.

I decided to take a tour to Italy. My friend, Tony, dropped me off at Chicago's O'Hare Airport and I remember clearly how scared I felt. He waved good-bye and I had a flashback to when I was five years old and my mother dropped me off for my first day at kindergarten. Thirty years later, there I was feeling just as small and alone. Yet my fear slowly gave way to excitement, sort of like it does when a roller coaster car begins that first big climb.

My fear didn't kill me and neither did my trip alone. I made an effort to put aside my natural shyness and met lots of nice people. I enjoyed wandering around towns by myself during breaks from the tour. My confidence grew as I realized that I could venture out into the world alone and get along just fine. There was now no question in my mind that I would continue to travel alone.

In the years since then, I've traveled alone twice more to Italy. Also to France, Greece, Yugoslavia, Argentina, Costa Rica, Singapore, Malaysia, Canada and many destinations in the USA, including Hawaii. I learn more and more with each venture; not only the mechanics of how to do it but also how rewarding it can be. I find it much easier to meet people and make new friends when I am on my own. Alone, I can submerge myself in a country, feel its rhythms, and learn its culture.

I began teaching adult evening classes called "Travel Alone And Love It" at two schools in Chicago. Interest was high and both classes filled. I was asked by both schools to teach again the following semester. Several private organizations have asked me to speak before their groups as well. I see what a tremendous amount of interest there is in the subject of solo travel. The age span of my students is early twenties to early seventies. Some are married but most are either single, divorced or widowed.

Solo travel was initially a scary choice. It has grown to become my preferred choice. It is not for everyone, but if you were interested enough in the subject to pick up this book, then it is probably for you.

I am not advocating anything daring, rough or adventurous. I have never carried a backpack or stayed in a youth hostel, though perhaps someday I will. I am cautious about the places I choose to visit alone. There are some areas of the world where, because I'm a woman, I would be more comfortable and secure with a companion. I do travel safely, cleanly and on a modest budget. You certainly may have more leeway than I do as far as budget goes, but I think you get my drift. My style of travel is pretty mainstream. It's suitable for anyone who loves to explore new places and meet new people. And, it's suitable for anyone who refuses to let the lack of a compatible travel companion keep them home.

In the following pages, I'll give you detailed instructions on how to research, plan and accomplish your own successful solo journey. My goal in writing this book is to give you the knowledge and confidence you need to travel alone and love it.

Anticipation

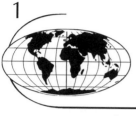

Why Travel Alone?

Why do we choose to leave home, where everything is familiar and comfortable? Why do we spend hard-earned vacation time and money and endure long hours of travel to arrive at a place that is foreign? What is the allure of different people, strange surroundings, peculiar food, odd customs, maybe a foreign language?

Travel speaks to our souls and feeds some primal hunger. What's around the next bend? What's over the next hill? We feel more alive when we see a place for the first time and let all the new sensations wash over us. This is the joy of discovery. It's why subsequent trips to a place can never quite match the wonder and thrill of that initial visit. But there is a more common and basic explanation for our wanderlust. It is our universal quest for knowledge and understanding.

What lies beyond that which we already know? As we travel, our unspoken questions are always, "What is it like to live here?" and "In what ways would I be different if this had been my home?"

We want to learn as much as we can about the places we visit. We're drawn by history, politics, important sites and physical treasures. But we crave the opportunity to connect with other people. We want to understand their values, their customs, what they eat, how they eat, what they wear, their sports and their music. We're fascinated by the differences we find and heartened by the things we have in common. Connecting with people in this way lifts us spiritually. It helps us to see ourselves differently…as a part of something much greater than our usual sphere. We feel in our souls that we are truly citizens of the world. We sense an interconnectedness with the people we meet, in spite of cultural differences that are sometimes great. In learning more about a different country, its people and their culture, we also learn more about the world, about human nature and, ultimately, about ourselves.

The best way to learn about other people is to mingle with them. The more direct contact you have with the people of another culture, the more you will learn. You will not be able to do this while you are traveling in a group of twenty or thirty other Americans. In a group, you will simply be a tourist. You will see the sights you are supposed to see. You will be herded into restaurants, handicraft factories and "folkloric dance" halls, all of which churn countless, faceless hoards of tourists through their doors. There is no time or effort wasted on personal interaction; if you've ever been on one of these tours you know exactly what I mean. You will form opinions of the place based on what you observe, which will be superficial at best. But you will not know the place or its people unless you find time to go off on your own for awhile.

With a little courage, you may eschew the tour and decide to see a place with a friend. I've done this many times and almost always enjoyed the experience. But I've found that I've always returned knowing a lot more about my friend and very little about the place we've just visited. Why? Because we always had each other to talk to. It was easier for us to talk to the person we knew than to strangers. Wrapped up in the pleasure of each other's company, we felt no need to make the effort.

It's quite a different story when I travel alone. With no one I know to talk to, I actively seek conversations with new people. Sometimes I ask for directions, advice or assistance, but just as often I seek a simple friendly exchange.

Furthermore, we are more approachable when we're alone. For example, if you came upon a pair of tourists in your own city, you would be reluctant to intrude on what you observe as a companionship between them, even if they ask you for directions. You would give them directions and assume that they neither want nor need your company. Yet you may readily offer conversation, further assistance or even an invitation to someone who is alone. There's a tendency to want to take the person under your wing. As a solo traveler, I am often the beneficiary of this compassionate human trait.

Don't confuse traveling alone with being alone. Sure, you may have a few fleeting moments of feeling lonesome, but consider them a tradeoff for those moments of impatience you have while traveling with a companion. When traveling alone, we greatly increase our probability of meeting people. In all my travels, I've found people more willing to strike up conversations and offer help and companionship to me as a solo traveler than when I've been accompanied. The world has become a more neighborly place for me because I've learned I can count on the kindness and friendliness of people wherever I go.

The more one-on-one conversations you have with people of the country you're visiting, the more you will learn; about their country, its people and their beliefs. You will be a traveler, not just a tourist. You will come home with insight, not just photographs!

Another reason to travel alone is freedom. I mean freedom from ever having to say, "Oh, I don't care, what do you want to do?" This is your vacation, time and money.

Of course you care. Traveling alone means never having to compromise. You alone choose exactly where to go, when to go, where to stay, how long to stay, and what to do while you're there. Tailor your vacation to your specific desires. There are no schedules to keep. You might have a tentative schedule in mind, an idea of things you'd like to see and do, but you are free to improvise and act on impulse. It's a very intuitive form of travel. Invitations and opportunities will arise and you can decide which to pursue.

Usually I am a "city person." I love visiting cities to see what people have built for themselves in the way of architecture, museums, parks and restaurants. I take advantage of the entertainment available whether it's theater, jazz, or street musicians. But sometimes I'm in the mood for relaxation. That's when I'm drawn to the great beauty and serenity of Hawaii or the Greek Islands—two of my favorite travel destinations. There is plenty to see and do, but the atmosphere is conducive to leisure.

Occasionally I travel alone because I need solitude. In my job as a flight attendant, I work with literally hundreds of people each day in very close quarters. I love my job but sometimes I get burned out and need a stretch of time to just be by myself. So I will take a solo mini-vacation. Sometimes I will escape wintry Chicago in the dead of January for a few days of warmth and sunshine in Florida. On these trips I pack lots of books along with my journal. I rarely speak to anyone, preferring the peace of silence and my own company. Twice I've rented a cottage for a week in Michigan. It was a rickety old cabin high on a bluff overlooking Lake Michigan, just a two hour drive from my home. It was inexpensive, a factor always important to me when I'm alone. But its main appeal was that it had no telephone or television. I filled my car with books, my ever-present journal, candles, my coffeemaker, beach chair, and my boom-box with lots of classical CDs. In the mornings, I'd sip coffee and write at a table next to the front window of my cottage. I couldn't see the lake because of the heavy growth of trees and bushes, but I'd enjoy watching the birds, squirrels and chipmunks. In the stillness I could hear the waves lapping at the bottom of the bluff. I'd take long walks down country roads, prepare simple meals from fresh produce sold at roadside farm stands and read good fiction while lazing on my beach chair. Solo travel of this sort restores my soul.

Normally, though, I'm in a "people-person" frame of mind and actively seek the company and companionship of others.

Solo travel allows you to match your trip to your mood.

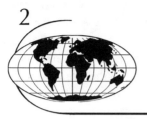

Overcoming Fear

> *"Life shrinks or expands in
> proportion to one's courage."*
>
> ANAIS NIN

If solo travel is so wonderful why aren't we all doing it? Fear!

Many people tell me, "Wow, you're really gutsy. I could never travel alone, I'd be too afraid." Yet they can never tell me what it is they fear. Perhaps their fears run the gamut... fear of dying... fear of getting sick, hurt or lost... fear of crime... fear of being lonely... fear of losing their luggage... fear of having no one to turn to for help. Or maybe they are simply frozen with fear at the thought of doing something they have never done before.

Let's take a look at fear itself.

Webster's dictionary defines fear as "an unpleasant emotion caused by expectation or awareness of danger." We can all agree that fear is an unpleasant emotion. It can even cause physical side-effects such as trembling, dry mouth, and butterflies in our stomachs. And fear is certainly caused by an expectation or awareness of danger! Yet fear is often present in our lives even when there is no expectation or awareness of danger.

For example, when I learned that I was accepted by two schools to teach my class, "Travel Alone And Love It," I felt all the physical manifestations of fear that I've just described. Yet I knew that there was no danger involved in teaching the classes. I was familiar with the schools and the neighborhoods; one is just blocks from where I once lived. In fact, I'd attended classes there many times myself. So why was I afraid to teach? I could think of only one reason. I'd never done it before.

My panicked thinking ran along the lines of, "Oh my God, what have I done? I don't know anything about teaching—I pour coffee for a living! I could really screw this up! I might stand up in front of a room full of strangers and make a fool of myself! What was I thinking?"

I eventually calmed myself down, hearing a wee small rational voice in the back of my mind saying, "It'll be okay, you know your subject very well. All you need to do is prepare and practice."

Fear comes up throughout our lives when we have the courage to try new things, set new challenges, expand our comfort-zone. We must do the things we want to do in spite of the fear if we want to conquer that fear.

I recommend a book that discusses this subject in depth, *Feel The Fear And Do It Anyway*, by Susan Jeffers, Ph.D., published by Fawcett Columbine. Susan writes, "Whenever we take a chance and enter unfamiliar territory or put ourselves into the world in a new way, we experience fear. Very often this fear keeps us from moving ahead with our lives. So many of us short-circuit our living by choosing the path that is most comfortable."

In the coming chapters I will talk a great deal about how to avoid danger and keep yourself safe and healthy. It is important to ensure that any fear you may have while traveling alone is based on inexperience, not danger. That kind of fear is normal and it's okay to feel it. Just don't let it slow you down. Your fear will even be useful to you when you travel alone; it will keep you alert and cautious. It will also motivate you to be well prepared. Because a part of that fear is of the unknown, it will help calm you to find out as much as you can about a place before you go.

Now let's go back and take a look at some of those fears we mentioned earlier.

Afraid of dying? Well, it's not likely this will happen on your vacation unless you are very unhealthy to begin with, or you do something very foolish. Otherwise, death will happen when it happens. There is a place in your passport for the name and number of whom to contact in case of emergency.

Afraid of getting sick or hurt? Your hotel or the U.S. Embassy can recommend an English speaking doctor for you to see. You may choose to purchase travel health insurance. You will sometimes get a nuisance ailment when you travel: blisters, a sore throat or a cold. Always carry medication just in case.

Afraid of crime? You are already living in one of the highest crime countries on earth. So you have the advantage of "street smarts" that many tourists do not have. Stay out of countries that hate Americans, stay out of bad neighborhoods and be alert. More about this in the "Personal Safety" chapter.

Afraid of getting lost? This is one of the most enjoyable things about travel! It can be delightful to wander off the beaten tourist path and make your own discoveries. It's also an excellent excuse to ask strangers for help. If you are in doubt about the safety of your surroundings, duck into a public place and ask. If it is not safe, find or call a taxi. Always carry the name and address of your hotel with you. Getting lost is wonderful! I highly recommend you do it on a regular basis.

Afraid of losing your luggage? I will talk about this more

in the chapter, "Protect Your Belongings," but let me assure you that, if the airline loses your luggage, they are also responsible for getting it back to you. Your most important items should be with you in your carry-on bag. You should not have packed anything of great value to begin with.

Afraid of being lonely? This is the irony of traveling solo—you are rarely alone. If you are at all open to meeting people, you will. You will meet other travelers and exchange thoughts on what you've seen and plan to see. You will also meet friendly locals who are proud of their town, city or country. They will gladly answer your questions. They may even offer to show you around. Sometimes I decline these offers, if I feel wary or if I just prefer my solitude. But generally I jump at the chance for some company and a personal tour.

Afraid of having nobody to talk to? When you travel alone, of necessity you will talk to other people all day long: "How do I get to this museum?", "Where is a good place for lunch?", "Is there a flea market in this town?", "Where are the best stores?", "Would you please take my picture with this camera?", "Can you recommend any good day tours?", "Is there someplace I can go to listen to live music?", "Is this the correct bus to take to get to the concert hall?", "Can you please let me know when I've reached my stop?" These simple pleas for guidance often lead to pleasant conversations. Sometimes, though, you'll be alone when you see something that thrills, awes or fascinates you. You'll wish you had someone to share the moment with. That is when it helps to keep a journal. I "talk" constantly to my journal. It is my permanent travel companion. I sometimes write for hours a day—at meals, in parks, at cafes, on my balcony at sunset, with a glass of wine or cup of coffee. I record the events of the day, my thoughts and feelings. I describe my surroundings, including the people I meet.

Afraid of having no one to turn to for help? Solo travel will restore your faith in humanity. You will be amazed to find that help is everywhere you need it. Help is often offered before you have time to ask! When people see you are lost or confused they invariably offer assistance. I have never been disappointed.

No matter how much research we do and how well we prepare, life and vacations will take unexpected turns. But these events usually add richness to our experience, teach us some lesson and become our most vivid memories. I cannot promise you that nothing bad will happen when you travel alone, any more than I can promise you nothing bad will happen if you stay home. But I will show you how to do everything possible to make your journey a safe, joyous one.

Chicago's beloved basketball superstar, Michael Jordan, taught us a valuable lesson when he embarked on a baseball career. Here's a man who has nothing to prove. He could easily have retired and relaxed for the remainder of his life, secure in the fact that he achieved everything possible in his chosen profession of basketball. He has fame, glory and lots and lots of money. But Michael knows that life is much richer when we set goals. Life is more meaningful when we challenge ourselves. Few people took him seriously when he announced his goal to play professional baseball. There were many vocal skeptics. Amid all the scoffing and skepticism, Michael said, "I've never been afraid to fail. I'm strong enough to accept failure. But I couldn't accept not trying."

If your goal is solo travel, then you must proceed toward that goal. You mustn't accept not trying. Start small if you want—take a tour to a nearby town—but do start. Courage is not the absence of fear, but proceeding in the face of fear.

This is life. It is temporary. You can stand fearful at the edge or you can jump in.

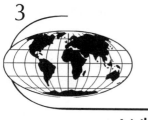

Where to Go

What a delightful dilemma! You have the world to choose from. You may already have some places in mind.

It will help you to keep a travel file. Maintain a separate folder on each potential destination. Whenever you read an article about a place that sounds interesting, clip it out and file it in a folder labeled with the name of that city, state or country. I get most of my clippings from travel magazines and the Sunday newspaper's travel section. Some articles may have general information about what to see and do in an area, others may be about one specific aspect of a place such as its food, the entertainment or handicrafts. Many articles are about towns and villages that are off the beaten path and, therefore, more interesting and often less expensive. When your friends go someplace great, have them bring back brochures, maps and any other information that could help you. When people recommend good hotels and restaurants or tell you the perfect place to shop for souvenirs, write this all down and add it to your files. You'll have a head start in knowing which places interest you, as well as lots of practical information on hand. Then you'll begin the process of prioritizing and narrowing down your choices.

You are restricted only by time, money, safety considerations, your taste in destinations and your own level of travel experience.

Experience Factor

Let's talk first about your level of travel experience. If you have never traveled alone, maybe you feel a little scared. We each go through life trying not to scare ourselves too much, comfortable within our envelope of security. So where you decide to go depends on how much you are willing to stretch that envelope. How much of a cultural change are you ready to experience? How much independence can you handle?

Nobody expects you to trek through India if you've never left Indiana. If you're truly timid or inexperienced, then start small. Take this in baby steps. Try visiting a nearby city or take a weekend drive through the countryside. Let your confidence begin to grow. Each small achievement will prepare you for the next.

If you don't feel ready for full independence, by all means sign up for a tour. You can always wander off from the tour for short periods to test your wings.

Are you not ready to visit a country where English is not spoken? That still leaves you the United States, Canada, Great Britain, Ireland, Australia and New Zealand. The province of Quebec, Canada would be a good place to hear another language, French, yet still have the safety net of English readily available.

From there it is just a small cultural hop to Western Europe, where English is widely spoken and the customs and food are similar to our own. Your next step toward the more exotic might be Eastern Europe, Mexico, Central and South America, all of them still fairly similar to our own culture.

Ready for a still greater change? Then it's on to Asia, Africa, and India. The world is yours, brave soul! Again, start with a tour if you would like some extra guidance and support in a radically different culture.

Safety Factor

Call the State Department before you decide on an overseas destination. The current phone number for information is 202-647-5225. You will be greeted by a recorded message which will guide you through instructions to obtain information on the country or countries you are interested in. You will be given information about what travel documents you'll need as well as any health problems and safety risks you should be aware of. You'll also be told what types of crime are prevalent and whether there has been any recent terrorist activity.

I recently called the State Department to help me decide whether to go to Singapore and Malaysia, or to Istanbul. I was warned of terrorist attacks on tourists in Istanbul. Several people have told me how wonderful Istanbul is and how there's really nothing to worry about, but, a) I'd be all by myself, b) my own government is warning me, and c) why should I subject myself to this risk? It is a very big world with many places to visit. Please avoid placing yourself in unnecessary danger from terrorists or serious outbreaks of disease.

Istanbul is still on my list of places to see, but I'll wait until it is safe. The State Department reports on Singapore and Malaysia, on the other hand, warned only of pickpockets and credit card fraud. I had a terrific time in both countries.

Time Factor

How many vacation weeks do you get each year? Do you take them all together or do you prefer to split them up? One week is enough time to visit another city in our own country, to enjoy a sun-filled vacation in the Caribbean or a beach vacation in Mexico. But allow at least two weeks if you plan to see more of Mexico, or if you want to go to Europe, Central or South America. A minimum of three weeks should be allotted for travel to Asia, Australia, New Zealand or Africa. The more time you spend in one place, the better you will come to know it. Try not to pack too many destinations into one trip. When can you go, versus what is the best time to go. Many people, for instance, would say that summer is the best time for a European vacation. I disagree. Europe is infested with tourists in the summer. That's when airfares and hotel rates are at their highest, the hotel and restaurant people are harried and every other person on the sidewalk is carrying a map and camera. The weather is still delightful in Spring and Autumn when school is in session, rates are lower and the people who live there have more time to talk to you. So try to aim for the "shoulder" season if you can, as opposed to the "high" season.

Money Factor

If you love travel as much as I do, I strongly suggest setting aside a certain amount of money each payday that is earmarked for travel. Perhaps you could authorize a direct deposit into your credit union or money market fund for this purpose. It is best to have this money saved ahead of time so that your vacation won't be spoiled by thoughts of huge bills when you get home.

What kind of vacation can you afford? Some countries are more affordable than others, and our dollar is stronger against some currencies than others. It pays to keep abreast of these matters by talking with travel agents, reading travel magazines, business publications and both the travel and business sections of your newspaper. The business section publishes rates of exchange against other major currencies and tells us if the dollar is up or down against the Japanese yen and German mark, for example. Even when the dollar is weak against most of the world's currencies, there are always exceptions. When our money has a lot of purchase power in Canada, Mexico, Thailand, Poland, and Greece, that's the time to go to there. Two of my recent vacations have been to the Greek Islands and Canada.

Find a good travel agent to help you arrange the best airfare. You may want to ask your agent to compare fares to two or three different destinations you are considering. Pricing is not logical and it may cost you no more to fly across the country than it does to fly across your state. Early birds are rewarded by buying cheaper fares far in advance. Be sure to inquire about charter flights, too. Airfares to many overseas destinations drop in September after school is back in session

Do be sure to take advantage of the frequent flyer programs which are offered by airlines. You accrue credit for the miles you fly, which can then be exchanged for free flights. You may request an application for each airline's program from their ticket counter or their ticket sales office. You may also enroll over the phone by calling the airline's reservations number. Certain credit card companies and even telephone companies are now offering frequent flyer miles to their customers.

Next, you'll need to compare prices for food and lodging. Food and lodging in Greece, for instance, are very inexpensive. A two week vacation in Greece may cost no more than a one week vacation in New York. You can do some research in a travel book store such as Rand McNally, or in any bookstore with a good travel section. Look through the guidebooks for the destinations that interest you. Look in the table of contents for the sections on food and accommodations. Most books list restaurants and lodging in several budget categories. From these, you will get an idea on the costs of sleeping and eating in each destination. Once you decide on a destination, you can go ahead and purchase the guidebooks that most appeal to you.

Then you must ask yourself what degree of luxury and comfort you require. With a limited budget, would you choose two nights at the Ritz... or three weeks at a hostel? I, personally, prefer the longer stay, but want something a little nicer and more private than a hostel, so I fall somewhere in the middle, opting usually for an inexpensive hotel for two weeks.

Is it important for you to have a private bathroom? Many old, European hotels do not have a bathroom in every room. It is, of course, less expensive to stay in such a room. There may be one bathroom on each floor that is shared by the people staying on that floor. Is it important that your hotel room have a television? Or, that your hotel have a concierge or tourist desk?

"Bed and breakfasts" are popular in some areas, and "homestays" are available in others. In some cities, Prague and Budapest come to mind, many families earn extra money by renting spare rooms to tourists. I traveled through Yugoslavia for two weeks staying in people's homes—I always had my own key and my own room—for fifteen dollars or less each night. This type of lodging will not only save you lots of money, it will give you a first hand glimpse into their way of life. Tourist offices in each city can help you locate these rooms, or sometimes you'll see signs in the windows of such homes. Sometimes people with rooms available may approach you or hold up signs in airports and train stations to get the attention of potential customers.

What is your dining pleasure? This will also determine how much your trip costs. Can you eat local food in simple surroundings? Or is it important to revel in fine cuisine along with music, candles, flowers and white tablecloths? Obviously, the simpler your taste, the lower the cost.

Lunch is always less expensive than dinner, so you might try making lunch your big meal of the day and opt for a sandwich, soup or salad for dinner.

Choosing your destination is just the first of many fun decisions you will make!

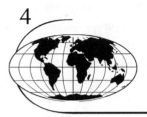

To Tour or Not to Tour

The ideal is solo independent travel. It allows you to immerse yourself, however briefly, into another culture.

I feel comfortable traveling independently to many countries because I'm an experienced traveler. Yet, for more exotic places I've never been to, like India and Africa, I would not hesitate to take a tour.

You must ask yourself some questions. How independent are you? Do you sometimes enjoy dining, shopping, walking alone? Do you feel self conscious when you're alone? Do you meet people easily? Are you confident of your ability to take care of yourself ? Have you been to your destination before? Is its culture radically different from your own? Do you have the motivation and time to read about your destination in advance and make your own plans?

For my first solo trip I chose a tour because I was nervous about traveling alone. I figured that, if something happened to me and I didn't show up one day, at least someone would come looking for me. I chose a tour of Italy. It was a nice, friendly group and I had a good time. On the other hand, it didn't take me long to realize that I could easily have gone to all the same places independently. It would not have been very difficult for me to find inexpensive rooms or to travel by train between cities. I do not speak Italian, but I noticed that the Italians who deal with tourists all seem to speak at least a little English. I felt the need for more free time to explore, make my own discoveries, chat with the locals and sit at cafes. At one point, I was on the bus with my tour group traveling from one city to the next. From my window I watched a train running on tracks parallel to the highway, heading in the same direction. I tried to imagine what it was like on that train filled with people speaking Italian. How I wished I was there mingling with the Europeans instead of on my bus with the Americans.

I do not regret that first tour. It was my "parachute," enabling me to test my wings without fear. It built my confidence so that I was able to later travel independently throughout Europe.

There are advantages and disadvantages to package tours.

Advantages

- You have the security of others to rely on. You'll always have someone to talk to and look after you.
- Everything is prearranged for you—flights, hotels, sightseeing, often even meals and entertainment.
- You need not worry if you are afraid of a language problem. You will never have to speak to anyone but your tour guide and fellow tourists.
- You can make friends with other people in your group.
- You can take what I call a "buckshot" tour (it goes all over but does not penetrate deeply) for your first time in an area. You'll see a lot of places in a short period of time. This will give you an idea of places you'd like to return to on your own and see at a much more leisurely pace.

Disadvantages

- Most tours are, like Noah's Ark, arranged for pairs. In the fine print of tour ads you'll read that prices are based on a per-person, double occupancy rate. You'll pay a single room supplement that can add hundreds of dollars to the cost of your tour. A few tour companies will offer to find you a roommate for your trip, which will save you from paying the single room supplement. Ask your travel agent about these. Then you must, of course, ask yourself how comfortable you would be rooming with a stranger. Tours usually book you in nice, well located first class hotels that are large, impersonal and cater to tour groups. By traveling independently, you can stay in small, inexpensive, privately owned hotels with few or no amenities but in a decent part of town. You will save money and get a better feel for the country you're in.

- It is impossible to immerse yourself in the local culture while you are with twenty other Americans! You will observe from a distance and be just another tourist. The few locals you do meet will not see you as an individual, but as one of a herd. The waiters, hotel staff and shopkeepers you meet will be too busy servicing your group to have time for one-on-one conversation with you. You'll miss out on the little moments of understanding that occur when two people from different cultures "connect" with each other by sharing ideas.
- You will have no freedom to linger in the places you love or to leave early the places you don't care for.
- You have no control over who else may be on your tour. They may be too young, too old, too noisy, and there seems to be a law that there is at least one whiner on every tour. I was once on a tour bus when two men almost got into fisticuffs over whether to open a bus window.
- Your days are planned for you and many of them start very early. You are often given instructions such as, "Have your suitcase packed, outside your hotel room door by 6 A.M. and be on the bus by 7am." If, like me, you're not a morning person, this could seem more like work than vacation.

Veteran traveler Charles Kuralt says, "Most travelers are timid. They should be a little braver. I would never go on a tour, even if I were going to Tibet or some place I'd never been. I like going on my own and relying on the friendship of strangers, which always seems to come. No matter where you are, when people see you're puzzled, they always try to help. And I think the chance for a memorable trip is greater if it's not an organized one."

My advice to you is that, if you prefer to do a package tour, try to find one that includes lots of free time, perhaps one with just your airfare and hotel included. Your travel agent can help you find a tour that's right for you.

A compromise alternative to the package tour would be to sign up for a series of short tours when you get to your destination. Every major city has at least one tour company offering half-day, full-day and evening tours. Many even offer tours of two days or more to surrounding areas. By taking these tours, you won't feel you've missed any important attractions, yet you'll not feel like part of a herd twenty-four hours a day. And you'll still be able to take advantage of more inexpensive hotels.

If you travel independently, I do recommend taking one or two short sightseeing tours, especially the ubiquitous half-day city tour. These short tours are a great way to get the lay of the land, quickly see the highlights of a city, decide what places you'd like to come back to on your own and meet some fellow travelers who are often from different countries themselves. On a recent trip to Singapore, I signed up for a half-day sightseeing tour and met Trish and Jeff, a delightful young couple from Melbourne, Australia. I enjoyed their company and learned more about Australia in the process.

In any case, I strongly recommend that you allow yourself plenty of time to explore a place alone. Learn as much as you can through your own direct impressions and your own direct contact with the people.

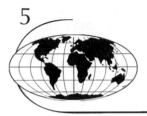

How to Prepare

Your preparation should begin as soon as you decide exactly where you want to go. I like to allow at least three months for preparation so I don't feel pressured or rushed. Your goal is to find out as much as you can about the place. You'll feel more confident about going alone when you know what to expect. Let this be fun!

There are many sources of information. An enjoyable way to start might be to rent a video about your destination; many video rental stores carry travel videos. Check your travel file for any information you already have on hand. Talk to people whom you know have been there. Even if your friends haven't been there, perhaps they know someone who has. This will give you some practice in talking to strangers. Besides, most people are happy to share information about their travels. Be sure to take notes.

Your library will have travel books, magazines and maybe even video tapes. Copy or take notes from the pertinent information.

Finally, you must select guidebooks for your destination. Find a travel bookstore like Rand McNally or at least a bookstore with a large travel section so you'll have many books to choose from. Plan to spend some time leafing through the books before deciding which ones most appeal to you. Each book has a slightly different focus and style. Every travel writer has his or her own point of view and it will benefit you to get more than one opinion. For this reason, I find it important to buy at least two different guidebooks. This also gives me different sources of information that I can compare on hotels, restaurants, and things to see and do. Sometimes I'll splurge and buy three or four books.

The *Adventurous Traveler Bookstore* catalog has listings of hundreds of travel books and maps, most with a strong emphasis on adventure travel. Many of the books are about hiking, climbing and biking, but some of the books will be of interest to any traveler. Poring through this catalog will give you many vacation ideas and arouse your wanderlust. To obtain a catalog you may call 1-800-282-3963, fax 1-800-677-1821, E-mail: books@atbook.com.

Selecting a guidebook is a personal matter. Your choices may differ from mine. I typically stand in the aisles for at least an hour looking through the entire selection of books for my destination. I pore through each book, gleaning more and more information as I do, before I narrow down my choices. I'll usually choose one that's small, lightweight and packed with pertinent information on sightseeing to carry with me during my travels. I'll choose another with lots of color pictures to give me an idea of what I'll see when I get there. And I'll usually also choose one for the budget traveler, filled with suggestions on where to eat and sleep inexpensively.

People often ask me which are my favorite guidebooks, but I really can't recommend one over another. Each is valuable in its own way. My own travel bookshelves are crammed full and the selection runs the gamut. Let me describe for you some of the brands you're likely to find in any good bookstore.

Fodor's is a great general guide for places which you will be visiting for the first time. It gives you lots of planning information such as when to go, how to get there, what it will cost and tour information. It gives you the addresses and phone numbers of the country's tourist offices where you can call or write for further details such as maps and hotel information. It recommends hotels and restaurants for every budget. You'll get a brief rundown on the history, cuisine, and culture of the country, a few translations of handy travel phrases, and many practical hints for your travels there.

Frommer's is another comprehensive guidebook. I have two versions of Frommer's; one is their compact *City Guide*. The other is their *$ A Day* guide, such as *Greece on $35 A Day*. Keep in mind, though, that the $35 figure is based on two people traveling together and sharing lodging. Your expenses as a solo traveler will be higher because you'll be footing the entire hotel bill, but these are still great guides for the budget traveler. You'll find descriptions of all your possible destinations as well as a synopsis of history. I like their hotel and restaurant information. They also have a small section of phrase translations.

The *Frommer's City Guide* is also a very comprehensive guidebook with lots of practical information as well as a brief historical profile. Their hotel and restaurant information are listed for every budget category.

Berlitz also gives us a choice of guidebooks. Their pocket size combination travel guide/phrase book has a large section of translations organized by color and according to topic. The travel guide section covers the basics of history, what to see and do, as well as what to eat and drink. It does not have hotel and restaurant information, but its compact size makes it perfect to tuck into your bag to refer to as you sightsee.

The *Berlitz Travellers Guides* are created for the experienced, sophisticated traveler. They don't have a lot of "how to" information for planning your trip, but they do offer wonderful descriptions of each place with brief mentions of some of the hotels and restaurants.

Let's Go guides are written for the budget traveler who is young or at least young at heart. They are all inclusive guides that cover history as well as all the practical information you need to plan your trip and get around. They also offer the usual info on everything to see and do. I especially love these guides for their wealth of information on budget hotels and restaurants.

Insight Guides are noted for their beautiful photographs. More than a hundred color photos in each book grant us a sneak preview of the country we'll soon visit! Unlike many guidebooks, *Insight* places great emphasis on the people and the culture of each country. This is an advantage to you, the solo traveler. It offers you greater understanding of the people you'll meet during your stay there. Practical travel information is condensed in the back thirty pages or so of each book. The number of photographs and the fact that the book is printed on high quality paper make these guides too heavy to pack, but they are enriching to read before you go and a joy to look at anytime.

Michelin *Green Guides* are great for those who crave details on the sights they'll see. You'll get a brief rundown on history, and no information on hotels and restaurants. But you will find page after page of maps, drawings and tiny print describing in great detail everything there is to possibly see. The various sites are rated with stars as to how high they should be on your travel itinerary—from three stars which means "worth a journey" to no stars which means "see if possible."

The *Lonely Planet* guidebooks contain a wealth of practical information that is particularly useful to the solo traveler, especially one who is on a tight budget. In addition to the usual info on history, climate, geography, what to see and do, there are subchapters titled, "Dangers & Annoyances," "Women Travellers," and "Health." I appreciate the honest appraisals, details and practical information in these intelligent guides.

Try to keep in mind that your guidebooks are a tool, but not a crutch. Use them to help you but don't let them control you. Study them for general ideas and information, but be brave enough to find your own discoveries too.

Once you've purchased your guidebooks begin reading them, absorbing information and highlighting the most important items. I treat this job as a fun version of homework. I'm not afraid to mark up my "textbooks," turning down corners and drawing stars or arrows in the margins. Pay special attention to the sections on history and government. This type of information gives you insight into the background and culture of the people you'll meet.

Because of their weight and the space they'd take up in your luggage, you probably won't want to pack all your guidebooks. I usually choose one to bring with me, using its blank pages to jot down important information from the other books. Another option is to use a copier to print the most important pages of the books you don't pack. A more drastic measure is to rip out just the most important pages to bring along. If you do this carefully, you can remove a chapter with the pages all still held together at the spine. Use a staple for added strength in keeping the pages together.

The appendix of this book contains a list of tourist agencies for many countries around the world. Phone or write to the agencies of the countries you'll visit. Ask for any additional information they can give you, particularly a map, hotel listings and information on any special events that will take place during your visit. They may also be able to send you restaurant listings and information on transportation, weather, museums and sightseeing tours.

Read about the currency of the country you'll visit. What is it called? What denominations does it come in? What are the coins? Check your newspaper or bank for the current exchange rate.

Learn how to read a map if you don't already have this skill. You can practice with a map in your own town before you leave home.

Read about the various attractions and highlight those that appeal to you most—cities, beaches, museums, cathedrals, historical sights. Decide what, for you, is "not to be missed." It's helpful, for instance, to have an idea of what towns you want to visit so that you can figure out the best means of transportation to get there. You'll read about the attractions each town holds for you and get a feel for how long you'd like to stay there.

Be realistic about how much you'll have time to see. I would rather explore a small area and get to know it well, than to wear myself out trying to see many places in a short amount of time. Allow yourself "free" time: to sit in cafes, to write your thoughts, to talk to people, to wander through parks and down side streets.

While strolling through a park in Warsaw, I happened upon a man of retirement age who stood patiently still, like a statue, holding a small tin of birdseed in his outstretched hand. He whistled and waited and, to my amazement, tiny songbirds flew out of the nearby bushes to feed from the tin in his hand. Just yards away was another old man feeding squirrels that climbed onto his arm. I was so happy to have shared in that moment of beauty and peace.

Make a tentative itinerary for yourself. But don't let the itinerary become your master. Invitations, opportunities and whims of fancy will arise that you should feel free to act upon!

Book your flights. Give your travel agent plenty of time to find the best deal for you. Three months is not too far in advance, but try to allow at least a month. "Special fares" do not apply to every seat on an airplane, and the cheap seats sell first.

Book your hotel room for the first night or two. You will be groggy upon your arrival and it is a welcome relief to know where you will be staying. You can always change hotels after that if you find someplace you like better. Use suggestions in your guidebooks or travel file. This is when it's great to have more than one source of information. Sometimes the name of a hotel in my price range will be recommended in more than one book and I will feel confident beginning my search there. I will usually call the overseas hotel directly, sometimes starting as early as 6 A.M. to take advantage of lower phone rates, while still catching the hotel during their business hours. Most hotels now have fax lines, so that is another way to make your reservation. You can always have your travel agent book your hotel for you, though I've found that the most inexpensive hotels are not often listed with travel agents.

Fantasize! As you read your books and articles, picture yourself there. What do you imagine yourself to be doing? Where do you see yourself? Museums? Parks? Cafes? Concerts? Cathedrals? What are you wearing? Are you smiling? Are you talking with people? Let yourself daydream and enjoy the vacation before it even starts.

There is yet another way you can prepare yourself for traveling alone: get used to talking to strangers. The bigger the town you live in, the odder this may seem to you. We are more respectful of each other's space and privacy in big cities. We cautiously avoid making eye contact. But this can also give us a feeling of isolation and loneliness. We are each traveling alone through life, in one sense or another. Reach out to some of your fellow travelers with a smile, a nod, a pleasant hello, a comment on the weather, a question or a compliment. Spread a little good cheer.

When someone asked Mother Theresa how people without money or power can make the world a better place, she answered, "They should smile more."

Safeguard Your Health

Vacations can be stressful. Plans to make, planes to catch, hotels to book, sightseeing, meeting new people, sampling new food. It's all a great deal of fun, but nonetheless wears us down a bit. The stress of travel can lower our resistance to illness, but there are things we can do to safeguard our health.

First of all, lessen the stress by beginning to plan your trip at least a few months in advance as I've suggested in the "How to Prepare" section. Do your research so you know what to expect. Do not try to cram too much sightseeing and activity into too short a time. Build leisure time into your schedule; time to occasionally sleep late, time for an afternoon of people-watching at a sidewalk cafe, time for a stroll through a park, and time to record your thoughts in a journal. Leave space in each day for quiet moments in which to recharge your battery.

Secondly, be sure you're healthy before you go. If you were going to drive your car across country, you would first check the tires, brakes, lights and engine. Show as much mercy to your body. Take care of any squeaks and rattles before you leave. If you regularly take prescription medicine, make sure it's updated and that you have an ample supply for your trip. If you have diabetes, epilepsy, severe allergies, or any other potentially serious but not obvious health problem, get a "Medic Alert" bracelet or necklace made for yourself. Paramedics know to look for these if you should lose consciousness.

Get in shape! I'm not talking anything drastic here, just that you be able to walk at least five miles a day. Maybe not all at once, but in shorter distances spread over the course of a day. Not that you're going to do that every day of your vacation, but I firmly believe that walking through a city is the best way to really know it. You will notice things that you never would see from a bus or car window. You'll discover charming squares, beautiful gardens, interesting architecture, neighborhood restaurants and unique shops. You'll get a better sense of each different section of town as you walk around.

Do you take a good multiple vitamin daily? I'm no health expert by any means, but I rely on people who are for my information. See if you can find a good health food store in your area. Talk to the people who work there and find someone who seems to be knowledgeable. Then pump them for information. Ask about melatonin, the latest jet lag remedy, which is supposed to have many other health benefits as well. Some brands of vitamin supplements are better than others, some combinations are more effective than others, so seek the advice of experts.

We've all heard of the health benefits of vitamin C. But there are other supplements that can help us, too. I learned that garlic is believed to strengthen the body's immune system. You can buy "sociable" garlic supplements that won't make you reek of garlic odor. I take these daily when I'm on vacation and a few times a week when I'm home. Another great "find" is acidophilus, the active bacteria culture that is found in yogurt. You can buy it in supplement form. Some of it needs to be kept refrigerated, but some brands are stable at room temperature. Acidophilus is a "friendly" and very helpful bacteria. Apparently our bodies are just crawling with all sorts of bacteria (this is normal and okay), but acidophilus helps to keep the "bad" bacteria in check. This can be especially important when you travel, as it may help to prevent diarrhea, constipation and stomach upsets.

Make sure your diet is high in fiber—fresh fruits, vegetables and whole grains—and be sure to drink plenty of water. You'll see most flight attendants, including myself, carrying around a 1.5 liter bottle of mineral water. Actually, it starts out as a bottle of mineral water, but we keep refilling the bottles from drinking fountains in airports and hotels. The airplane water is drinkable, but not the greatest. It's put into the airplane's water tank through a hose on the ramp outside the jetway.

The water is safe to drink in most of the countries you're likely to visit, such as those in Europe, yet many Europeans buy bottled water to drink instead. The same thing is happening in the United States because, I suppose, of a slight distrust of the purity of our tap water and a desire for water without additives, such as chlorine. The point is to drink at the very least 64oz. of water each day. Flying dehydrates you, so you'll need to compensate by drinking even more while you're aloft. Drinking out of the 1.5 liter bottle is a good way for us to keep track of the quantity we consume. A minimum one and a half bottles of water a day should do nicely.

At least eight weeks prior to your trip, find out if you need any inoculations or antimalarial medication. Your guidebooks will probably mention it if you do. Just to be safe, especially if you're going someplace a little off the beaten path, call the Centers for Disease Control in Atlanta at 404-332-4559. Is there any risk of getting hepatitis A at your destination? If so, ask your doctor about the recently approved vaccine, Havrix. If you do need any shots, get them early. Some inoculations take as long as eight weeks to achieve their full protective capability. You'll be given an official yellow booklet, the International Certificates of Vaccination with the dates and types of your inoculations recorded within. You should put this with your passport and take it with you.

If you will be traveling to a place where mosquitoes will be present, it is believed that taking the vitamin supplement thiamine, or B1, will help repel them. Taken at 100mg three times a day, the amount your body doesn't absorb is exuded through your pores. Mosquitoes and flying insects don't like the smell and tend to stay away. Can't hurt to try it, but I would certainly also use a regular mosquito repellent with 20% of the active ingredient called "DEET" (N, N diethyl-meta-toluamide). This is especially important if you are traveling to an area where malaria or dengue are present.

Make yourself a mini first aid kit. Mine is in a medium size zip-lock plastic bag. It contains aspirin, strip bandages—especially the tiny ones for blisters, throat lozenges, decongestant, a very mild over-the-counter sleeping pill, earplugs and some small packets of alcohol swabs. You may also want to include some antibacterial ointment, Imodium-AD for diarrhea, and, if you are sexually active and not in a monogamous relationship, you may consider including some condoms.

Each of us has our own physical weakness; a certain ailment we invariably come down with when we're under stress. Mine usually starts with a sore throat and grows into a head cold, chest cold or laryngitis. With all my careful precautions, though, it has been many years since I've had worse than a sore throat while on vacation. Think about your own physical vulnerabilities—what breaks down first for you—and be prepared to fight the symptoms if they occur.

While on vacation, continue with your health regimen. Continue taking your vitamins and other supplements. If you don't want to take acidophilus supplements, I recommend trying the yogurt in whatever country you visit. You'll find many different kinds that we don't have at home. In Costa Rica, for example, you'll find yogurt made with the delicious fruit, guanabana. In Greece you'll find a rich, creamy yogurt so thick you can stand your spoon up in it. It's served with honey and sometimes also walnuts.

A number of books offer information on staying healthy while traveling. One excellent and extremely comprehensive guide is *Travelers' Health, How To Stay Healthy All Over The World*, by Richard Dawood, MD. Another good book which is small enough to take with you, should you desire, is *Health Guide for International Travelers*, by Thomas P. Sakmer, MD, Pierce Gardner, MD, and Gene N. Peterson, MD This pocket size guide contains some specific information for each country.

Avoiding Travelers' Diarrhea in Developing Countries

If you are traveling to a "third world" or developing country there are extra precautions that you must take. In addition to shots and antimalarial medication, you must be especially careful about everything you eat and drink. The motto is, "Boil it, cook it, peel it or forget it." The problem is the water. You cannot rely on purification of the water in these countries, so you must not only avoid the water, but also everything that has come in contact with the water. Drink only bottled or canned water and, even then, make sure that the bottle or can is still sealed when you receive it. Do not even use tap water to brush your teeth or rinse your mouth. This means that you must also avoid ice. Soft drinks and beer, straight from the bottle or can are safe. Alcohol does not kill all bacteria, so mix it only with bottled or canned beverages without ice.

Eat only in reputable hotels and restaurants. Trust your guidebooks for this information. You must still avoid salads and fresh fruits that have no peel. No raw food washed in tap water is absolutely safe. It is best to eat steaming-hot foods, cooked foods right off the fire, citrus fruits that you peel yourself and dry foods such as breads and crackers. Avoid food served by street vendors. Dairy products are not pasteurized in some parts of the world. If in doubt, avoid milk, butter, cheese and related products.

Dr. Rebekah Wang-Cheng, Associate Professor of Medicine at the Medical College of Wisconsin, recommends Pepto-Bismol for traveler's diarrhea because "it actually helps kill the toxic bacteria in addition to slowing down the volume of stool." She also suggests taking along an antibiotic such as Bactrim or Cipro for "tourista."

I've only had food poisoning once and it was my own fault. I went into a coffeeshop in Lisbon with a dear friend who was with me on that trip. We were tired and wanted something sweet with a cup of coffee to perk us up. But this place was not especially clean and it was swarming with flies. Patsy selected a piece of chocolate cake and I chose something that looked like it was angel food cake with orange sauce, but tuned out to be a soft meringue with a sweetened egg yolk sauce. It had not been refrigerated (see what I mean about it being my own fault?). It didn't even taste good, but I unconsciously picked at it as we chatted away and ate the whole darn thing. It took about six hours for the pains to start, and then, well, I won't go into it. I stayed sick for the rest of the week, able to eat only boiled rice, tea and bullion. My friend had to leave for home. My original intention had been to stay and explore more of the country on my own. That would have been impossible, so I just cut my losses and returned home for help from my doctor.

I'm telling you this sad story just to warn you to be very careful where you eat as well as what you eat! With precautions and common sense, you should not have to worry about getting sick on your vacation.

7

Personal Safety

Safety is my highest priority. None of us likes to feel scared and vulnerable, especially when we are alone. It undermines our confidence and can spoil our full enjoyment of a place. No place is one hundred percent safe, not even your own home. But some places are safer than others. This is why it is so important that you do your research on a place before you decide to go. In this case, ignorance is not bliss. By not knowing the status, you could inadvertently place yourself in a potentially dangerous situation.

Inform yourself. Read at least a couple recently published guidebooks. Read newspaper articles that mention current events in the country. Find out the political situation of the country. Is it stable? Do they have friendly relations with the United States? Do they like Americans? If you are a woman traveler, you need to know what is the prevailing attitude toward women. Would a woman alone be looked at with suspicion? Is a woman alone likely to be harassed or shunned? What is the economic condition of the country? Is there widespread poverty or high joblessness that could lead to a high rate of crime? What kind of crime is prevalent? Is there any crime directed toward tourists? Are there any active terrorists organizations? Have there been any terrorists acts directed toward tourists?

Your most important source of information is, of course, the United States Department of State. You may listen 24-hours a day to consular information and travel warnings by calling 202-647-5225. You may receive the same information by fax by dialing 202-647-3000 from a fax machine. Or you may receive the information in writing by sending a self-addressed, stamped envelope to: Overseas Citizens Services, Room 4811, Department of State, Washington, DC 20520-4818.

If you call the phone number you will get a recorded message telling you to punch in the first four letters of the name of the country you are inquiring about. Then you will hear a recorded message telling you whether you will need a passport or visa, any unusual currency or entry conditions, unusual health conditions, the crime and security situation, political disturbances, areas of instability and drug penalties. The Department of State also gives addresses and emergency telephone numbers for U.S. embassies and consulates.

After you gather all this information, you can make an informed decision as to how safe you would feel in this country. If the answer is, "not very," then do not go there. It's as simple as that. It's a very large world with many places to see. It is not difficult to find a relatively safe place to visit, so do not risk placing yourself in danger. I, personally, have decided not to visit countries where terrorist activity and rampant street crime are present. Granted, street crime is a big problem right here in our own cities, but I'm at an advantage here, knowing the "lay of the land," knowing our customs and knowing the language. Nor will I go someplace where a woman alone would be frowned upon or harassed. It's unfortunate, because I am so curious about other cultures. The more different they are from ours, the more they fascinate me. I hate to limit myself, but I don't want to be a victim or feel like a victim, so I'll steer clear, at least until conditions change. Perhaps you are braver than I am and more able to tolerate risk. If so, then you should, as a precaution, stop in and register with the U.S. Embassy in the country you visit. The State Department and probably your guidebooks will give its location.

The State Department also publishes very informative booklets such as "A Safe Trip Abroad," "Your Trip Abroad" and "Travel Tips for Older Americans." You may call 202-512-1800 or write to the Superintendent of Documents, U.S. Government Printing Office, Washington, DC 20402. The booklets run from $1.00 to $1.25.

Once you've decided on a country to visit safely, there are many other safety precautions that you should take beginning with your packing.

First of all, no expensive-looking or designer luggage. You don't want to appear wealthy even if you are. Do not bring more than you can easily handle by yourself. Your luggage tags should be the covered type so that your name and nationality cannot be easily observed by strangers. You may choose to use your business address and phone number for your luggage tags. Lock your luggage and never, ever leave it unattended.

If you have made a tentative itinerary for yourself, make a copy to leave at home with a friend or family member, including any hotel information you may have. Phone home periodically to let someone know where you are and what your next plans are.

Do not pack any clothes or jewelry that could identify you as an American. We are all rightfully proud of our country and of our flag. But to some people, the American flag might just as well be a bulls-eye target. So do not advertise your nationality. Be selective about whom you tell you are American. Don't be too scared by this—use your instinct. Ninety-five percent of the time I don't hesitate to tell the people I meet that I am from Chicago. Years ago, the reply was invariably, "Oh, Chicago—Al Capone!" Now the response is usually, "Oh, Chicago—Michael Jordan!" However, if I were talking to someone who made me feel uneasy, I might instead say, "I'm from Toronto." Nobody seems to hate Canada.

Be selective about whom you tell you are alone. About ninety percent of the time, if someone asks, I tell them that I'm traveling alone. Usually they're a little surprised, then curious and a nice conversation ensues. If, though, I feel a bit wary about the person I'm talking to, I offer one of several stories: "I'm with my husband who's here on business," "I'm here with a tour group, and I must leave now to meet them," "I'm meeting my friends here later today." You get the idea. Prepare for yourself a mental list of "escape" lines and be ready to use them if you ever feel the need.

Try not to advertise the fact that you are a tourist; dress conservatively in style and color, do not walk around with a camera hanging off your neck and don't stand in the street reading your map. If you are lost, duck into a shop, cafe or doorway to look at your map. When you're on the street, though, try to look like you know what you're doing. I usually fold my map into a small square, showing just the area I'm exploring, and keep it in my coat pocket. If I need to refer to it, I can do so without looking obvious, because the map is then only the size of my hand.

Be very careful about giving the name of your hotel to strangers. Often when I'm at work, passengers ask me what hotel we stay at in a certain city. I never let them know. Most likely they're simply curious, but it would be a security risk to tell them. Instead, I'm just vague, "I can't remember the name, but it's right downtown." That always seems to satisfy them.

When you meet someone nice and would like to get together with them again, arrange to meet them somewhere rather than have them come to your hotel. When you know them well enough to trust them, you can tell them where you're staying. You must feel reasonably sure they're not a terrorist, opportunist, gigolo, rapist or thief. Men can be fooled by inviting a woman to their room for a night of romance, then waking up to find their wallet and watch gone. If your "people instincts" are not so finely honed, then it's safest to remain cautious.

Be careful to limit your alcoholic intake to what you can handle and still be alert and able to exercise good judgment. If someone were to see you drink your third or fourth cocktail, they might decide that you look like a easy target.

Make sure that your hotel is in a safe area. You can usually trust your guidebook's recommendations, but see for yourself what kinds of businesses surround the hotel. Usually there are other hotels, restaurants, coffee shops and stores. Be wary of any hotel that is in an area of sex shops, vacant lots, vacant buildings or factories.

Avoid staying in hotels with direct access to your room from outdoors. I occasionally make exceptions to this rule if I feel comfortable with the surroundings. Avoid rooms on the ground floor so you can rule out anyone trying to break in through the window. Avoid rooms adjacent to the fire exit stairwell door, in case "stranger danger" chooses to lurk there.

Does the hotel seem clean, well lit, friendly and competently run? You may ask to see the room before you decide to take it. I do this when I am searching for inexpensive rooms in small family run hotels or guest houses.

Do not let the desk clerk announce your room number within earshot of strangers. If they do, you should ask for another room and quietly explain why. You may have a bellman escort you to the room, but, if not, do not prop the door to your room open with your suitcase while you check it out. I see flight attendants do this all the time. It's not so bad when there is a group of us together in the hall, but could be dangerous if "stranger danger" is watching. Believe me, he is not hiding under your bed! He would be lurking in the hall waiting for you to unlock your door so he can push his way into your room with you. If you do see a stranger in the hall and you feel wary, do not open your door. Go back to the front desk and report him. If you don't want to tip him off, you could pretend to be visiting someone and just knock on the door, then leave when there's no answer. I don't mean to scare you, this has never happened to me. It's just smart to have a mental game plan for any odd occurrence.

Don't get into an elevator with a suspicious looking person. When you get into an elevator, try to stand next to the control panel so you can punch all the stops if you need to. If you feel uncomfortable about the person with you in the elevator, pretend you forgot something and go back to the lobby rather than getting off on your floor.

When you're in your room, use all the locks provided. Make sure that all your doors are locked before you turn in for the night, including windows, adjoining room doors and sliding glass doors.

Small hotels overseas may not have much in the way of security so you might consider packing a portable door locking device. These fit in between the doorjamb and the door, and prevent the door from being opened from the outside even by someone who has a key. I've recently begun packing one of those little personal security alarms. I can carry it with me when I'm out walking, keep it next to the bed when I sleep or use a special attachment to wedge a sensor between my closed door and the door frame. If the door were opened, the alarm would go off.

In a pinch, you may need to use your ingenuity. A few years ago I stayed three nights in a private guest house in Santorini in the Greek Islands. My room, owned by a married couple who lived upstairs, was attractive, immaculate and only $16 a night. But by day three it was clear that the husband's interest in me went beyond that of a kind host. I discouraged him in no uncertain terms. I was nervous about staying there that last night but it was too late to find someplace else. So, I placed a chair against my locked door and balanced a drinking glass on the edge of the chair. I knew that I would awaken if the glass broke on the marble floor, scream to scare him and awaken his wife. Then she could come down and help me clobber him!

What would you do if a man wearing a workman's uniform knocked on your door and said he's there to check your air conditioner? Give yourself a pat on the back if you said, "Call the front desk." Do not open your door for anyone that you have not invited. The correct response is to ask the man to wait a minute, then call the front desk to verify that this is legit. We had a flight attendant attacked at a New York hotel by a man dressed in a workman's uniform who told her he was checking all the heaters. Luckily she managed to escape. Now, if you've ordered room service and twenty minutes later a person knocks on your door with a tray of food, you have my permission to open the door. (I did hear of one flight attendant who makes the waiter identify what food is on the tray before she'll let him in!)

I usually keep my room key, or key card, in my wallet. Don't leave it out where anyone could read the room number. In many small European hotels, the room key is attached to something about the size of a brick and almost as heavy. These keys are meant to be left with the desk clerk when you go out. I don't think it's the safest way to operate, but that's the way they do things. I trust that if they had problems they would change their policy.

Do not use the "maid service" sign on your door, because it indicates that the room is vacant. Maids will come in anyway to clean your room. They'll knock, then enter at a time you are likely to be gone.

Be very nice to the entire hotel staff. You'll rely on them for safety and for information. Ask the desk clerk for a map of the area, if you don't already have one. Ask him or her to mark on your map the location of the hotel and any areas that you should avoid. Find out about local transportation. Is it safe after dark? Ask for the name and address of your hotel written in their language. This will help you to get back if you get lost.

When you are out and about, be alert, not fearful and not caught up in daydreams. Be aware of your surroundings and the people around you. Do not use your cassette player because it will distract you from your surroundings. Ignore any Romeo's, whistles or cat calls, just as you would at home. Be more cautious after dark. Find out in advance from your hotel staff if a location is safe at night as well as what is the best way of getting there and back. If I have a specific place in mind, I usually check with the desk clerk to make sure that it is "respectable" for a woman to go there alone.

If you ever find that you've accidentally wandered into a questionable area, go into a public place and check your map or call for a taxi. In Philadelphia on a layover, I went for a long walk alone. I suddenly found myself in an area where everyone but me had tattoos, purple hair and lots more than two earrings each. I know how Dorothy felt when she landed in Oz. I ducked into a coffee shop and talked to a nice young man there. I explained that I was from out of town and asked if I was safe walking around that neighborhood. He assured me that I was, then marked the areas to avoid on my map.

Stay in well lit areas with other people around. If you find yourself in a fairly deserted area at night, walk close to the curb or even in the middle of the street, away from dark doorways and alleys. I did this in Prague. I'd walked to a concert when it was still light outside and the area was bustling. The walk back through deserted, unlit streets was eerie. I trotted back in the middle of the street! I've even done the same thing at home. I feel safer dodging a car than a mugger.

Blanche DuBois, in *Streetcar Named Desire*, said, "I've always relied on the kindness of strangers." When you travel alone, you will too. When you're out and about and you need some help, whom should you ask? Well, just about anyone, but here are some of my tried and true suggestions of people who can help you:

- Hotel staffs. Duck into the nearest hotel and ask the bellman or desk clerk for help.
- Shopkeepers, particularly of souvenir shops. I was once hopelessly lost in Venice. There seems to be a rule there that no street is allowed to go more than fifty yards without changing directions and names. My map did not show all the tiny streets so I asked the shopkeepers to point me in the right direction.
- Restaurant waitstaffs are usually able to help.
- Other tourists. You'll know who they are because of their maps and cameras.
- Students. Look for high school aged kids, as they've probably studied English.
- Business people. You'll know them by their suits, briefcases, and perhaps newspapers under their arms.

I mention the above people because all of them are likely to speak some English. But certainly feel free to ask help from anyone you feel comfortable with. I have never been disappointed. My only caution about this would be to the lone woman traveling in a culture where women have little independence. Here, if you approach a man for help, your "boldness" could be misinterpreted. It would be better for you to approach women instead.

It restores my faith in humanity that people everywhere have been so kind to me and helped me whenever I've been lost or confused. I have even had people go so far as to take me where I'm going.

This happened to me most recently in Kuala Lumpur; twice in one morning. I was walking to the Handicraft Center on my first day there. The streets, a jumble of cars, motorbikes, fumes and noise, are not well marked. I asked a young man for directions and he was going that way so he walked with me. At the Handicraft Center, I bought a beautiful framed batik print. I planned to carry it back to my hotel, then continue shopping. The sidewalks were crumbly, bumpy and not easy to walk, especially carrying my large print. I couldn't find street signs to check my whereabouts so I asked instructions from a woman who was selling sharksfin soup at a hawker stand. She didn't understand English, but got a man to help me. That man, Tom, drove me to my hotel. He was with a small group of men when he offered the ride, and, seeing the wary look on my face, they assured me, "He's okay! He's good man!" So I took the chance. It turned out that he needed to drive in that direction anyway. I sure hope so, because the traffic was awful. He was very kind.

One exceptional example of kindness happened to me in Milan. I arrived there by train around eight-thirty at night and the tourist information office at the station had just closed. I had intended to book a hotel room through them. I reverted to "Plan B" which was to call one of the hotels listed in my guidebook. I got out my book, found a phone, but could not figure out how it worked. (It's always an adventure using pay phones overseas because they all work differently. With some, the coin goes in before you dial, some after—and they make different sounds for ringing and for busy signals.) I looked around for help and saw a middle-aged man standing nearby who was of slight build, wearing glasses and carrying a newspaper. I correctly pegged him as a businessman. He spoke just a little English, but understood my problem. He helped me place a couple calls, but the hotels I tried were full. I ran out of change, so he used his money until he, too, ran out of change. He said, in fractured English, "Come with me, I will drive you to my office which is in the area where you want to stay. We can make more phone calls from my telephone there. Then I'll take you to whatever hotel we find for you." Wellllll… I know that the State Department and my parents would frown on this, but I accepted his kind offer. My instincts were right that, a) he was sane, b) he was a very kind man, c) he was a gentleman and, probably, d) he was flattered to aid a damsel in distress. It helped in my decision that I was bigger than him.

We made just one phone call from his office and found a room within my budget at a one-star hotel in an excellent location nearby. He drove me to the hotel and carried my suitcase in for me. I was only staying for two nights and I was going to Verona for the first whole day, but I asked if I could treat him to lunch the following day. He accepted. When Riccardo met me, he had his delightful secretary with him because she spoke fluent English and could help with conversation. He insisted on treating me, not only to lunch but also sightseeing! We saw the Cathedral, the opera house, and DaVinci's "The Last Supper." Then he bought me a bouquet of daffodils, drove me to the train station and said good-bye. It was a wonderful, magical, Cinderella day for me.

It's not a typical instance of the kindness of strangers, but it sure was fun and I wanted to share it with you.

When you get help from strangers, it's a pretty safe bet

that you can trust someone whom you approach. After all, they weren't lying in wait for you. They were just going along minding their own business. It was you who interrupted their life, not the other way around. But be more wary of someone who approaches you until you can get a feel for their intentions. Are they sincerely trying to help, or are they hitting on you, or possibly setting you up for a robbery? Be prepared with one of your escape lines if you're not sure. "My boyfriend, 'Killer,' is meeting me here any minute."

I hope that you're not frightened after reading this whole chapter on safety precautions. I'm sure that you already knew about most of them. If you currently live in any city in this country, you already have some "street smarts." Crime statistics show that you are already living in one of the most dangerous countries in the world. Just about anyplace else you go will be safer. Great consolation, right? Guns are less prevalent and crime is more "polite" in other countries. Here, if someone wants your wallet, they'll point a gun at you and demand it. Then they may shoot you anyway. In other countries, if someone wants your wallet, they'll try to take it without you knowing it. Isn't that nice of them? We can protect ourselves from pickpockets much more easily than from guns. So take a deep breath, relax, and I'll tell you all about protecting your belongings.

Protect Your Belongings

No matter where you go, there will be a few people who'd like to relieve you of your valuables. They don't really want to hurt you. They certainly don't want to go to a lot of trouble to get them. But, if your valuables seem easy to take, someone will try to take them.

So the trick is to make your goods harder to take than the next guy's. I have been to many of the world's pick-pocket capitals and have never been hit. Nor have I been scammed or robbed. Am I lucky? Sure! But I also know I'm not an easy target.

Just in case my luck runs out, I always make two copies of all my valuable documents: passport (the picture page), drivers' license, credit card, tickets, ATM card and travelers checks. I put one copy in my suitcase and leave the other copy at home with a trusted friend. That way, if any of these things are stolen they will be easier to replace. You could even go a step further by adding the phone numbers to call in order to cancel and replace these items.

Ninety-nine percent of the time you won't need to bring more than fifty dollars in U.S. currency. Just make sure you have enough to buy yourself some refreshments at the airport and to pay for your airport parking, if necessary, when you return. Don't worry about buying foreign currency before your trip; you can exchange a traveler's check at the airport when you arrive at your destination. Even though the exchange rate at the airport may not be as favorable as at a bank there, it is still cheaper than buying the currency in the United States. French francs will always be cheaper in France.

Take just one credit card, I suggest either Visa or Master Card—they are both widely accepted worldwide. A credit card will give you the best rate of exchange, but there will be times when only cash will do, so also take either traveler's checks, an Automated Teller Machine card or both.

ATM cards are becoming more popular worldwide. You'll want to check with your bank before you go to make sure you'll be able to use it at your specific destination. Ask if you will need a different PIN number or if your card has to be re-encoded. Find out if your bank charges a fee per transaction. Perhaps your bank could even provide a list of ATM locations for your destination. Be very cautious of where and when you use the ATM card, making sure that the area and the people around you seem safe. I feel most secure using ATM machines that are inside banks, though I would also use a machine on the street if it was in a safe neighborhood during daylight hours. Just duck inside someplace safe, such as a bank or hotel, to discreetly count your money.

Some ATM machines will accept credit cards for cash withdrawals, but be aware that your credit card company will treat this as a cash advance and charge you accordingly with a finance charge computed daily.

Sometimes it will be to your advantage to carry a few hundred dollars in small American bills. Are you traveling to a country where the currency is unstable and dropping in value? In this case, you may be able to negotiate very good deals on lodging and purchases by using our "hard" currency. Be sure to keep most of it hidden in a pouch under your clothing, putting into your wallet only what you'll need for that day.

Don't look wealthy! I've already suggested that you leave your designer luggage at home. The same applies to your good jewelry. A modest looking watch and a few simple pieces of costume jewelry should do nicely.

If you stay at a hotel, use their safe deposit box for the valuables such as tickets, excess cash and traveler's checks that you won't need for awhile. There is no charge for this service. Your things go into an envelope which you seal and sign, then into the safe. The methods vary for keeping track of your deposit. Sometimes you'll get a receipt, sometimes you must sign the deposit into a register book, and other times you may get your own key. Some hotels, such as the one I stayed at in Maui, have an individual safe in each guest's room. If you find you have one, I urge you to use it even if there's a daily charge for the service.

If you stay in a guest house or small hotel with no safe deposit box, then you must be more clever with your valuables. I suggest using the slim, lightweight pouches that are to be worn under your clothes. I have one that is worn over one shoulder with the pouch falling under my arm and another that goes around my waist or slightly higher.

The type of tote bag or purse that you carry plays an important role in protecting your belongings. I do not recommend fanny-packs for city use because they can be unfastened in a snap by anyone nearby who wants to take it. I don't like backpacks for city use either, because you have no idea what may be going on behind you. Someone with a razor could be slicing into your bag. However, in less crowded places where everyone has their own circle of space, a fanny pack or backpack will do nicely.

When you shop for a tote bag, look for features that make it safe for your belongings. Is it roomy enough to hold everything you'll need for the day? Mine measures

13" deep, 14" long, and 4.5" wide. This makes it large enough to hold my normal purse contents (hairbrush, lipstick, tissues, eyeglasses and wallet) as well as my camera, map, journal and small guidebook. Sometimes my umbrella goes in also. It's made of thick leather that would be difficult to slice through. It has two straps which would be difficult to cut. The straps are long enough to fit over my shoulder, but short enough that the bag hangs above my waist, completely under my protective arm. The bag zips all the way across the top so that no one can reach in. I always carry the bag so that, when it's zipped closed, the zipper pull is in front of me. I am in the habit of keeping the zipper pull in my hand, especially when I'm in crowds.

Keep your bag "attached" to you at all times. If you're sitting down, either keep the bag in your lap, put it on the floor between your feet with the straps over your knee, or put it on the floor next to your chair and sit on the straps. Never set the bag in an adjacent chair or hang it off the back of your own chair. If you want to sleep on a bus or train, use your bag as a pillow. Keep the straps wrapped around your wrist.

Men should be sure to keep their wallet in their front pants pocket to discourage pickpockets. When visiting cities overseas, odds are you will fit in better wearing a sport coat than you would a windbreaker, even with jeans. Then you'll be able to take advantage of all those nice inside pockets.

Be wary of any sudden commotion. Thieves often work in teams. One or more will divert your attention while the other steals from you. The diversion could be almost anything—a handful of coins dropped in front of you, a group of children pushing around you, something spilled on you or even someone asking you for help. Always be aware of your possessions when you are in crowds, stores, buses and trains.

Do you tend to lose things? I never used to, but I seem to be a few marbles lighter these days, so I find I need to concentrate more on keeping all my belongings. Last year I left my coat on an airplane and wasn't able to track it down until I returned home. Now I keep one of my business cards in my coat pocket with a note on the back to please call me collect so I can arrange to get it back. You could drop a card in your camera case as well, though my camera is always in my tote bag which I never let go of. I find that it helps to count the number of items I'm carrying. Then I remember the number and periodically take inventory, "Three. Let's see, coat, tote and suitcase. Great!" Because I no longer trust myself, I've developed the good habit of looking behind me whenever I leave a place. When I leave a hotel room, I always check one last time in the drawers, closet and bathroom.

Speaking of losing things, I'm sure you've all heard horror stories of luggage lost by airlines. If an airline loses your luggage, they are responsible for getting it back to you. If, at your destination, your suitcase does not roll onto the carousel with all the rest of the luggage from your flight, you must see a representative from the airline in their baggage claim office. You'll need to fill out a claim form and the airline will do a trace of your bag. They may offer you a complimentary toiletry kit or a small cash advance to buy a few necessities. If they don't offer, by all means, ask. Get a copy of the claim form as well as the name and phone number of the person who helps you. You may want to call daily to check on the progress of locating your bag. If the bag is forever lost, the airline is financially responsible, up to a certain dollar limit. For domestic flights the liability limit is $1,250, but it is only $650 for international flights. If you know that the value of what you pack is greater than that amount, then you should ask the airline about purchasing excess valuation coverage.

Many bags look alike so, to prevent someone from taking your bag by mistake, do something to make it unique. Put a bit of colored tape or yarn around the handle or use a distinctive luggage tag.

Make sure that the suitcase you check is securely locked. You can purchase combination locks for your luggage in travel stores and from many mail-order catalogs. The Brookstone catalog, 1-800-351-7222, has many helpful travel devices including bright red luggage locks with luggage tags attached. They also have a belt with a combination lock to place around your luggage. Many airlines, in their efforts to cut costs, have hired outside contract help for their baggage service and, unfortunately, theft is not unheard of. Remember, make your goods harder to take than the next guy's.

Of course, you will have no lost luggage worries if you can condense your belongings into two carry-on bags. And what a self-satisfied feeling it is to breeze through the baggage claim area, past all the people anxiously waiting to see if their bag will show up!

I've already advised you to steer clear of countries where you could be a victim of violent crime. Now I've shown you how to protect yourself from theft and loss. It's important for you to travel without fear. Just stay alert and aware and you'll be fine.

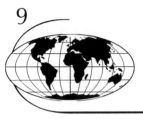

9

Travel Insurance

Do you need travel insurance? Let me help you decide.

Do you already have health insurance? Will your policy cover you while you travel abroad? What is the quality of health care in the country you'll visit? Is it top notch or sub-standard? If you became seriously ill or injured there, would you want to be evacuated to a place with better health care? Would you be able to access a large cash advance from overseas to pay for medical services in case of an emergency? Could you do this by means of your credit card, ATM card or money wired from family or friends at home? Hospitals overseas insist on full payment before you are discharged. They may hold your passport until they are paid.

If you take a tour and pay in advance, would you forfeit all or a portion of your money if you had to cancel? Would this be a major hardship for you? Would you like to insure yourself against your trip being canceled or interrupted due to circumstances beyond your control?

If your luggage is lost, stolen or delayed can you afford to replace everything yourself, or would you prefer that it be covered by insurance? Be aware that, if an airline loses (or destroys) your luggage, they are responsible for up to a certain dollar amount of the loss.

Would you like the assurance of knowing there is a number you can call from anywhere on earth and get assistance with any travel problems you might encounter whether it be lost travel documents, the need for legal advice or referral to an English speaking doctor?

I've researched the insurance coverage of eight companies, seven of which offer a menu of options from which you chose a package, the eighth, Traveler's Emergency Network, offers a set package. The prices are fairly reasonable, with current averages running about seven dollars per day. On the other hand, you could easily eat lunch for seven dollars per day. So you must weigh the tightness of your budget against the price for your peace of mind. You may buy insurance packages that are less comprehensive and, therefore, less expensive, or vice versa.

Typical Travel Insurance Options

- **Trip Cancellation and Interruption**: Provides reimbursement of non-refundable prepaid travel arrangements due to a number of reasons such as illness or injury to you or a close family member, financial default of a tour company or airline, strikes or natural disasters and your being required to serve jury duty.
- **Travel Delay:** Provides for reasonable additional expenses incurred due to a delay of twelve hours or more due to weather, labor strike, stolen travel documents or money, or equipment failure of your bus, plane or ship.
- **Baggage Delay:** Reimburses you for the cost of necessary items if your luggage is lost for more than twenty-four hours.
- **Baggage Coverage:** Reimburses you for covered loss, theft or damage of your luggage and its contents.
- **Emergency Medical Expenses:** Benefits are provided for expenses resulting from an accidental injury or acute illness.
- **Accidental Death or Dismemberment:** Provides coverage for death or physical loss of limb or eyesight due to accident.
- **Emergency Medical Evacuation:** Provides for necessary

transportation to a medical facility equipped to handle your special needs.

• **Worldwide Assistance:** The details differ per policy, but most generally include a phone number to call for medical and legal referrals, assistance with problems such as lost or stolen travel documents and the arrangement for emergency cash transfers through your credit cards, family or friends. Two companies, Carefree and Traveler's Emergency Network, also offer pre-departure services such as information about immunization requirements, weather, travel advisories and travel documents.

• **Dental Coverage:** Provides coverage for accidental injury or relief of pain. (Only two of the policies, Access America and Health Care Abroad, specifically mention this coverage.)

If you are not buying a tour, then you probably do not need trip cancellation or interruption coverage, as you will not have paid up front. If you are using only carry-on luggage, then you do not need baggage delay insurance and could well risk passing up the lost baggage insurance. If your current medical insurance will cover you for overseas travel and getting a cash advance overseas would not be a problem, then you may not need medical insurance. It is possible to pick and choose the coverage that most suits your needs.

Travel Insurance Companies

Access America
P.O. Box 11188, Richmond, VA 23230-1188
1-800-284-8300
OPTIONS:
• Trip cancellation and interruption
• Travel delay

- Emergency medical and dental
- Baggage delay
- Baggage coverage
- Accidental death and dismemberment
- Emergency medical evacuation
- Worldwide assistance

Carefree Travel Insurance

P.O. Box 247, Providence, RI 02901-0247

1-800-323-3149

OPTIONS:

- Trip Cancellation and interruption
- Travel delay
- Medical expenses — both accident and illness
- Baggage delay
- Baggage coverage
- Accidental death and dismemberment
- Emergency evacuation
- Worldwide assistance

CSA Travel Protection

P.O. Box 919010, San Diego, CA 92191-9970

1-800-348-9505

OPTIONS:

- Trip cancellation and interruption
- Travel delay
- Medical expenses — both accident and illness
- Baggage delay
- Baggage coverage
- Accidental death and dismemberment
- Emergency evacuation
- Worldwide assistance

Health Care Abroad (& Health Care Global)
(Wallach & Company, Inc.)
107 W Federal St., P.O. Box 480, Middleburg, VA 22117-0480
1-800-237-6615
OPTIONS:
- Trip cancellation and interruption
- Medical expenses
- Emergency evacuation
- Accidental death and dismemberment
- Repatriation of remains — pays to ship body if death covered by policy
- Dental expenses

Mutual of Omaha
P.O. Box 31716, Omaha, NE 68131-0716
1-800-228-9792
OPTIONS:
- Trip cancellation and interruption
- Travel delay
- Missed tour departure (due to weather delayed connection flight)
- Medical expenses
- Baggage delay
- Baggage coverage
- Accidental death and dismemberment
- Emergency medical evacuation
- Worldwide assistance

Traveler's Emergency Network
P.O. Box 238, Hyattsville, MD 20797-8108
1-800-275-4836
- This insurance is unique in having a set membership fee, currently thirty dollars, which is good for one year. There are no options; the coverage is fixed and includes,

among other things:
- Emergency medical evacuation
- Repatriation home when medically stable, if necessary
- Medical and legal referrals
- Transportation home for travel companions
- Return of mortal remains, if necessary
- Fast delivery of prescription drugs
- Cash advances of emergency medical expenses
- Pre-trip information
- Worldwide assistance

Travel Guard International
1145 Clark St., Stevens Point, WI 54481-2980
1-800-826-1300
OPTIONS:
- Trip cancellation and interruption
- Travel delay
- Missed tour departure
- Medical expenses
- Baggage delay
- Baggage coverage
- Accidental death and dismemberment
- Emergency medical evacuation
- Worldwide assistance
- Penalty waiver — pays half your penalty if you cancel trip for any reason
- Hotel overbooking — pays added cost of alternate hotel
- Special medical escort — if needed after accident or illness

Travel Insured International, Inc.
(The Travelers Insurance Companies)
P.O. Box 280586, East Hartford, CT 06128-0568
1-800-243-3174

OPTIONS:
- Trip cancellation and interruption
- Travel delay
- Baggage delay
- Baggage coverage
- Medical expense
- Accidental death and dismemberment
- Emergency medical evacuation
- Occupancy adjustment — pays extra room charge if roommate cancels

Be careful when you check out the various travel insurance policies. Read the fine print to know exactly what coverage you are and are not buying. For example, there may be a fifty to one hundred dollar deductible on medical expenses you incur. Some policies specify that their medical insurance will only cover emergencies, while others will cover more ordinary illness expenses. Must you show receipts or proofs of purchase for all items claimed if your luggage is lost?

If you decide against buying travel insurance and then become ill overseas, seek the help of your hotel staff or the US Embassy. They can help you find a doctor who speaks English.

Another service you may want to check out is IAMAT, the International Association for Medical Assistance to Travelers. It is a worldwide nonprofit organization of doctors, hospitals and medical facilities providing medical aid to travelers. They can send you, free of charge, the most current medical information, charts on world-immunization and a list of English-speaking member doctors and their phone numbers. Write for information to IAMAT, 417 Center St., Lewiston, NY 14092, or call 716-754-4883.

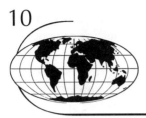

10

What to Pack

The fun begins! When you daydream about your upcoming vacation, envision where you'll be going, what the weather will be, what sorts of things you will be doing and what you'll be wearing.

When you're thinking about what clothes to take, there are two main considerations; climate and culture.

I recommend layers of clothing for travel. You can pile on the layers if you're cold and peel down when the temperature soars. Even the hottest climates sometimes have cool nights or overzealous air conditioning. A camisole, lightweight T-shirt or both combined make a good first layer. I almost always pack a black turtleneck sweater in cotton or silk knit. This looks good alone or layered under a cardigan, blazer or jacket. I have a photo of myself which was taken on a cold, damp Spring morning in Milan. I was wearing my black turtleneck (I wore a camisole underneath) with a beige cotton cardigan buttoned over it, a leopard print bandanna knotted around the neck, a black denim skirt and jacket, and black shoes and tights. A black and white lightweight wool tweed swing coat topped it off. The look was fun, stylish, warm and I could shed the layers as the day warmed up.

Try for a small mix-and-match wardrobe. You'll want most every top you bring to be wearable with most every "bottom," be it slacks or skirt or jeans. That way, you can get many ensembles out of just a few pieces. It's best to restrict your travel wardrobe to just two coordinating colors. A few different scarves can add pizzazz to this limited selection, changing the look from day to night as easily as changing from a red bandanna to a jewel-toned or leopard print silk. Men accomplish the same versatility with ties, and they take up so little room in your suitcase.

Think conservative when you pack for travel in countries other than our own. I cannot stress this strongly enough. We in the USA have one of the most casually dressed cultures on earth. We're used to it and we like it because it's so comfortable. But we must think differently when we travel, out of respect for the people and culture of the country we're visiting and so we don't make fools of ourselves, drawing unwanted attention. Strive to not look like a tourist. Do not, for example, pack shorts unless you are going to a beach resort. Even then, bring along more conservative clothes to wear when you leave the beach and go into town. You will not see anyone in Paris wearing shorts except for a few unenlightened tourists. Jeans, on the other hand, are universally worn by the young (and those of us who still try to fake it). Bright colors and bold prints or plaids will also help point you out as a tourist.

My travel wardrobe is predominantly black because it's sophisticated, conservative, doesn't show dirt or wrinkles and can be dressed up or down. I team my basic black with white or beige. I rely heavily on knits because they are comfortable, don't show wrinkles and can be easily rinsed out in the sink or tub and hung or spread flat to dry. There's no longer any need to lug along a travel iron when you go. A friend of mine cried, "But I don't have a body for knits!" Well, who does? We all dress for certain figure flaws, and I've found that most of mine can be camouflaged by wearing tunic length tops that are fairly loose fitting.

European men dress more formally than those in the

United States. T-shirts, for example, are seldom seen on city streets. Polo shirts, worn mostly for golf and other sports, are acceptable in conservative colors. Even in the summer heat, the stylish European will simply roll up the sleeves of his dress shirt. Men wearing plaid shirts with colored slacks, topsider shoes and nylon windbreakers are easy to spot as Americans. Those wishing to fit in will wear dark trousers, a long sleeved dress shirt and a sweater or sport coat in dark or muted tones. Jeans may be substituted for the trousers. Don't forget to include a tie for the nicer restaurants and clubs.

Women cannot go wrong wearing a skirt. They come in enough styles and fabrics that we can stay cool, comfortable and appropriately stylish. In modern countries, such as in western Europe, the length of your hemline won't matter, but in more conservative countries use discretion. Assumptions may be made about a woman traveling alone, and you don't want to play into that attitude by wearing mini skirts or any other body-conscious clothing. What is simply fashionable for us may be considered provocative in other cultures.

The climate in Singapore is very hot, yet, when I wore a sleeveless, long cotton dress, buttoned almost all the way to the neck, I noticed that none of the people who lived there wore sleeveless clothes. I did not receive any hostile stares, but I was happy that I did not dress any more casually. When I return to that part of the world, I'll know to wear clothes with sleeves. I've learned that I'm more comfortable when I compromise a bit on my own sense of style and comfort so as not to offend.

A friend of mine, visiting the United States from her home in Lyon, France, was surprised at seeing so many women wearing athletic shoes with their office clothes. I explained that women enjoy the exercise of walking to work in comfortable shoes, but they change into their dress shoes at the office. Needless to say, the custom has not caught on in France!

I occasionally see business women board my plane wearing athletic shoes with their business suits. I know sometimes we must walk for miles in an airport to get to our departure gate, but why spoil the look of an attractive suit with clunky white shoes? For travel, it's easy to find good, comfortable and attractive walking shoes—check out brands such as Rockport, Easy Spirit, Naturalizer, Soft Spots and Aerosoles. These companies produce very comfortable shoes in styles that are appropriate to wear with a skirt, suit or dress. Pack your sneakers, too, but save them to wear with jeans or khakis.

Two or three weeks in advance of my trip I start a running list of things to take. I carry the list with me everywhere I go because ideas sometimes occur to me when I'm busy doing other things. I add to the list and edit it as I get closer to D-day (Departure). There is nothing too small or too obvious to write on your list. I once almost left for Europe without my passport. So write down every item you intend to pack and check off each one as you put it into your suitcase, tote or purse.

Suggested Travel Wardrobe For Men

• Navy blue blazer
• Charcoal dress slacks
• Khaki slacks
• Jeans
• 2-3 dress shirts: white, blue and a pinstripe
• 2-3 ties
• 2 sports shirts: blue chambray and beige
• Turtleneck sweater in cotton or silk
• Lightweight pullover sweater to layer over shirts and/or under blazer
• Polo shirt: long or short sleeved

- Comfortable dress loafers
- Athletic shoes to wear with jeans
- 2 belts: one dress, one casual
- Raincoat

My Typical Travel Wardrobe
- Black knit straight skirt (knee length)
- Black knit tunic top with narrow white stripe
- Coordinating cardigan
- Black leggings or slacks
- Black flat-heeled shoes with rubbery soles (very comfortable but not too casual)
- Jeans
- Black turtleneck sweater
- Beige cotton cardigan
- Black polo shirt
- Two silk scarves and a cotton bandanna
- Black leather belt
- Athletic shoes (do not wear these with a skirt in any country but our own)
- Black leather tote bag (this becomes my purse when I'm on vacation)
- Small black purse for evenings

Depending on the length of my trip, I may throw in a couple more tops for variety that I can wear layered over the turtleneck, or alone with slacks or a skirt.

One advantage to traveling alone is that you can take your oldest, most dilapidated underclothes and pajamas (no one to see them) and simply throw them away when you pack to come home! That will free up more room in your luggage for new purchases you've made on your trip. I recently packed for a relaxing trip alone to Maui where I did a lot of writing, reading and walking. I packed a pair of athletic shoes with very little tread left, so those, too, were jettisoned before I returned home.

I always lay the clothes I intend to pack on my bed. This lets me visualize the various combinations I can make from the pieces I bring. I try to do this a few days before I leave so I can think about my choices and eliminate as much as possible.

Luggage

For my usual vacation of about two weeks, I'll normally take a 24" suitcase. Mine is a black softside nylon case with two sturdy wheels on the bottom of the back end and a retractable handle near the top of the front end. It's very easy for me to handle. I prefer nylon for its strength and light weight, softside because you can really cram it full, and black because it hides the inevitable dirt and scuffs.

I recommend that you avoid the "dogleash" type luggage pulls and luggage with tiny wheels on ball-bearings. I've had bad luck with these. The little wheels do not stand up well under the weight of a fully packed suitcase, especially if you're trying to pull it through the streets of Avignon, France from your hotel to the train station! My old suitcase fell on its side every time the wheels hit a crack in the sidewalk. Finally two bored teenage boys took pity on me and *carried* the suitcase for me, all the way to my train.

I have the airline check my large suitcase. The only things I carry onboard the plane are my tote bag, which I use as a purse, and a small additional tote bag for a bottle of water, my journal, books and any other items I'll want during my flight.

If I'm taking a shorter trip of, say, a week to ten days, I take just two carry-on bags, both in black. One is a 22" suitcase built on wheels with a retractable handle (the type you see all the flight attendants using) which fits in the overhead bin and under most airplane seats. The 22" size is the largest you can use as carry-on luggage. It has a detachable hook from which you can hang another bag. There are many versions of this bag in every price range. Look for one with large rubbery wheels as opposed to the cheaper hard plastic wheels which can crack. Some have the wheels on the narrow, side edge of the base. These bags tend to tip over on turns. Look for the wheels to be spaced farther apart on the wider, bottom edge for better stability.

The other carry-on bag I take is either a smaller tote bag with short handles that hooks onto the wheeled bag, or else a suit length nylon garment bag that I can hook over the pull handle of my wheeled bag. The garment bag is not reinforced and is extremely lightweight. It simply zips up around my clothes, which are left on hangers, leaving the hangers sticking out of the top of the bag. Luggage salespeople do not promote these because they are so inexpensive (less than $30 when I last checked) so you may have to request it. I've seen them sold in the "closet accessories" sections of department stores, in travel stores like Rand McNally, in discount stores like Service Merchandise and in the Lillian Vernon mail order catalog. Better men's stores give away vinyl versions of this bag to their customers who buy suits. Please do not buy those huge garment bags with all the outside compartments and a rigid bar across the center. Business travelers often carry these, and they board the plane looking like overloaded pack animals. Sometimes we flight attendants wonder if they're smuggling their families in these bags. There is not enough stowage space on planes for all of these "monster" bags and many airlines are restricting the size of those that may be brought aboard. Besides, they are just too heavy and awkward for you to carry as you travel alone.

My tote bag, which I use on vacations as my purse, is black leather and large enough to hold not only my normal "purse stuff" but also my camera (so I won't have the camera strapped around my neck pointing me out as an obvious tourist), my journal, a map, guidebook and maybe even a small bottle of mineral water. My current tote bag is fine in many ways except that it has no lining, so it tends to shed suede "lint" on everything I keep inside it. I'm always on the lookout for a perfect tote.

I'll include here a list of items that I normally pack for my trips. The list may vary according to my destination. I'm sure there may be at least one or two items on my list that may not have occurred to you, and you can probably think of one or two items you may want to take that are not on my list. If you can manage with less, then I envy you— you're a better traveler than me. Let this be a general guide for you.

What to Pack in Purse/Tote

These are the things you'll want to keep with you during the flight, though some of the "comfort" items like eye-shades, inflatable pillow and facial spray won't be needed for short flights of, say, less than three hours. Men might want to use a small nylon or leather duffel for these items. Wary travelers include one change of clothes just in case their luggage gets diverted.

- Any prescription medicine and eyedrops for dry eyes
- Passport case: mine is large enough to hold my passport, tickets, travelers checks, hotel info and immunization record book
- Small wallet: contains driver's license, one major credit card (Visa or Mastercard), ATM card, less than fifty dollars cash.
- Camera: you must decide whether you want to be a traveler or a photographer; it is hard to be both because a camera bag with changeable lenses marks you as a tourist. Your camera will make you a target for thieves. I've taken many great photos over the years with a discreet, pocket size camera that I keep either in my tote or in the palm of my hand. I frequently buy a souvenir pic-

ture book to supplement my own photos. If you're really into photography, perhaps you could compromise, taking your camera out for just part of each day and leaving it in your hotel the remainder of the time.

• Toiletries: Squeeze a little air out of your liquid containers to help counteract airplane pressurization changes.

• Large bottle of mineral water (1.5 liters). One for flights to Europe, two for Asia.

• Spray bottle of water for your face: refreshing, soothing, and your only source of humidity for the entire dry, dry flight. These come in various aromatherapy scents now.

• Luggage key

• Language phrase book or electronic translator (unless your guidebooks will have enough phrases to help you get by)

• Guidebooks (although I usually buy several to read before I go, I don't pack them all. I'll pack my favorite one—two if they're small. Then I Xerox the best pages of the others, or copy notes from them into the pages of the book I do take).

• Pocket calculator (not solar) for figuring exchange rates and prices

• Names and addresses of friends for postcards

• Journal: even if you don't normally write, solo trips are a great opportunity to start.

• Socks or "footies" to wear inflight: Wear shoes into lavs, though; just trust me on this.

• Tissues: bring your nice, soft ones from home. The ones on the plane are cheap and scratchy.

• Inflatable pillow which fits around your neck. (Use the airplane pillow to support your lower back.)

• Eyeshades to block out light and help you sleep.

• Earplugs to block out noise and help you sleep. (It is a little known requirement that every flight must have at least one screaming infant.)

• Tape or disc player, if music helps you relax and sleep on the plane. Otherwise, pack it in your suitcase.

What to Pack in Suitcase

• Wardrobe (don't forget undies and sleepwear)
• Umbrella (I had to pay $35 for the cheapest one I could find in Paris)
• Large bar of soap and washcloth
• Travel alarm
• Sewing kit (just thread a couple needles, put them through a 3x5 card and into an envelope)
• First Aid kit: Include items to treat whatever ailments your body is prone to. My kit fits into a medium ziplock plastic bag.
• Corkscrew: I love wine and enjoy trying the local ones when I travel. I often keep a bottle in my room so I can enjoy a glass before I go to bed at night.
• Clothespin (or large safety pin or paperclip). Great for closing drapes that don't quite meet in the middle, or for clamping closed a bag of snacks that you might have in your room.
• Liquid laundry soap in small container.
• Plastic bags in assorted sizes—for dirty laundry, camera film (take it out of those bulky cardboard boxes), soap and washcloth, wet bathing suit and all of your containers that hold liquids or lotions.
• Film—more than you think you'll need. I use about a roll a day.
• Extra batteries for your camera and tape player.
• Box of tissues. Most of the inexpensive overseas hotels I stay in have none. I always keep a fistful of tissues in my purse, sometimes to be used as toilet tissue. In public restrooms, sometimes there is no toilet tissue, sometimes it is of laughable quality, and sometimes you must pay an attendant for a measly amount. Toilet tissue overseas runs the gamut. I've seen some that looks like crepe paper and some that could double for

airmail stationery. I still have a strip of papery toilet tissue that I took years ago from a London loo that is printed with the words, "Please wash your hands!"

• Hair dryer, curling iron, electric shaver—if you pack these, then don't forget the electric converter and adapter plugs.

• Folded nylon expandable tote. Something to hold your extra purchases if you get carried away shopping. It lies flat in your suitcase if it's not needed. It's also great to use if you take a side trip and leave your large suitcase at your "base" hotel or train station.

• Book to read during quiet moments—at a sidewalk cafe, on the beach or in bed before you go to sleep at night.

• Xerox copy of all your documents (passport, tickets, travelers' checks, credit card, driver's license, etc.)

• Snacks: a little stash of trail mix, dried fruit or nuts in case you get hungry on a tour, in the night or when the restaurants are closed.

• Menu dictionary: I have these in French and Spanish, but, again, your guidebook may have enough phrases to help you.

• Hangers: sometimes I toss in a few plastic ones to use in case my cheap hotel doesn't supply enough.

• Supplies to freshen your manicure: at least clippers and an emery board.

• Wallet for foreign currency. The bills in some countries are much larger than ours and won't fit into our wallets, so I use a flat zippered case about 4x6.

• Tape player, tapes, (or disc player and discs) and mini speaker. I love music, and my tape player is also a radio. With the tiny speaker, I can tune in to local music or listen to my own tapes in my room while I shower and dress. I don't walk around town with it, though, because it would isolate me from the culture I'm there to observe.

• Tape measure: I pack a tiny one to help me figure out sizes when I shop for gifts.

• Candy to share: this is a recent addition to my list. I got
the idea from my father who brought a sack of tiny
candy bars (the type we give out on Halloween) with
him on our trip together to Poland and Czechoslovakia
(as it was then called). I smiled at the irony of this World
War ll vet bringing Hershey Bars back to Europe, but
they were a big hit and helped us make friends with the
people we met. Now, I always offer some to my hotel
staff and taxi drivers, also to children (with their parent's
approval) and anyone else I feel like sharing with. The
individually wrapped, bite size chocolate bars have been
popular. If there's a particular candy that is made in
your town, all the better. On my trip to Singapore and
Malaysia I took Tootsie Rolls because they don't melt in
the heat and they're made in Chicago.

• Your "life story." You will meet so many people when
you travel alone. They will be as curious about your life
as you are about theirs. I've found it very nice to have
photos of my family, friends and home. Include pictures
of your pets, your garden, and your hobbies as well as
postcards of your town and maybe even a small map of
the United States so you can point out where your town
is located. I carry my "life story" in a little plastic bag
inside my purse. Sometimes these pictures draw groups
of people who are curious. My "life story" has been
passed around train cars full of people from Provence to
Paris and from Singapore to Kuala Lumpur. These are
people who share my delight in learning a little more
about another culture. It's a great way to break the ice
and make new friends.

When you travel alone, you are not just a tourist. You
are an ambassador, an example to the world of what
Americans are really like.

You may be able to eliminate many of the things that I
choose to bring. If you can, you'll be better off. You may

also think of other things which, for you, are indispensable. That's why it's a good idea to start early in making your list and laying out the things you plan to take. Have a lot of fun with this, and do not obsess if you forget something. It is a great adventure to buy a "foreign" tube of toothpaste or bottle of lotion!

If you have trouble finding the right travel gadgets and accessories in stores near you, try shopping the mail order catalogs. An excellent source for travel accessories is the *Christine Columbus* catalog. Call 800-280-4775 or FAX 800-803-5383. The catalog is targeted for women, but most of the items in it are also fine for men. Another great travel catalog is *Magellan's,* 800-962-4943. Other good catalogs for travel items include *Brookstone,* 800-351-7222 and *Lillian Vernon,* 800-285-5555.

Sometimes the type of vacation will dictate a different list of what to bring. For example, when I went to Maui for a two week vacation, it was to write a portion of this book. I knew I'd have a room with a refrigerator and coffeemaker, so I brought a larger suitcase and packed it full of things to help me save money: boxes of cereal, nonfat dry milk and a plastic pitcher, a pound of my favorite coffee and filters, some crackers, a plastic bowl and flatware, herbal teabags, and a small container of dishsoap. I also brought along my laptop computer and books to read. I deliberately excluded my umbrella, knowing I would take advantage of rainy days to stay indoors and write.

While I'm on the subject of things to take with you, there are a few intangibles that I consider necessary for any traveler:

• Your best manners. You remember. Those little phrases our parents taught us when we were little: "Yes, please", "No, thank you", "Please, may I…", "Thank you very much", "Yes, ma'am", "No, sir", and on and on. My fellow flight attendants agree that the American public, over the last twenty years, has become more casual. Not only in their attire (boarding the plane in beachwear—tank tops, shorts, rubber flip-flops), but also in their manners. We see it all. People take their shoes off and put their bare feet on the bulkhead or the seat in front of them, they perform personal grooming in their seats (manicures, pedicures, plucking, flossing!), and they have forgotten all of those courteous phrases their parents taught them. Now we hear, "Give me a Coke," or "I'll take another bag of nuts." They give us their orders before we even ask, and the poking rate has risen; that is, people who poke us to get our attention (sigh), sad but true. One of these days I'll write to Miss Manners to get this all off my chest, but for now, thank you for letting me vent a little here. I only mention all this to caution you that people in most of the rest of the world still have their manners, so we all need to dust ours off and take them along with us when we travel.

• Your friendly face. Not the real serious one, not the scared one, the shy one, the impatient one or the one that no one can see behind. It's the alert one with the ready smile and nod for people who cross your path during the day; the face you wear when you enter a party knowing that many friends will be there. The face that expects good things.

• A sense of humor. I promise you that something will go wrong on every vacation. It will, someday, probably make a pretty good story. Sometimes we just need to take a deep breath and accept things. Laughter helps keep us sane in a world that often seems berserk. People are drawn to those who know how to laugh…especially at themselves.

> *"Resolve to keep happy, and your joy and you shall form an invincible host against difficulties."*
>
> HELEN KELLER

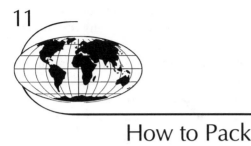

How to Pack

Relax! There's no wrong way to pack.

You should lay out everything you intend to take on the bed or the floor. Look through it all one last time to see if you really need to take all this stuff. Is there anything you could leave behind? Is there anything you're forgetting? Do you have that list handy of everything you intend to take? Check each item off the list as it goes into your suitcase, garment bag, tote or purse.

The big, hard or heavy things should go on the bottom. These include shoes, umbrella, box of tissues (don't be afraid to crush the box for more space), electric items with converters and adapter plugs, if necessary, and books not needed during your flight. Fit it all together like a jigsaw puzzle with the heaviest items at what will be the bottom when the suitcase is closed and standing up or being carried. Fill in the gaps with underwear and socks. Stuff small items into packed shoes.

When you pack bottles or tubes of liquids, creams and lotions, squeeze a little air out of the containers before screwing the lids on tightly. This will help counteract problems caused by the changes in pressurization during the flight. Double-bag in plastic all of these containers and pack them so that they will be upright when the suitcase is standing. You can bag several bottles or tubes together, just don't put two glass bottles together. I was glad I double-bagged the sun tan oil for my trip to Maui because it leaked out of the inner bag, but was contained by the second bag. The plastic bags could be as nice as zipped bags, or as tacky as grocery store bags just twisted and wrapped around the bottles. It doesn't matter as long as they prevent damage to your clothes if your liquids should leak.

The next layer you pack should be items that don't easily wrinkle or items whose wrinkles don't matter, such as the rest of your underwear, lingerie, bathing suit and T-shirts. Pack these items into the low spots left by the first layer. You want to create a more level surface for the top layer, which will be your nice outer-wear. I do not roll the garments—this does not prevent wrinkles and it makes your clothing take up too much room in the suitcase. Fold the items along the seams, where possible. The fewer the folds, the fewer the wrinkles. To prevent creases from forming at the knees of your folded slacks, pad the fold with something soft, like a sweater or two. To do this, pack the slacks across the length of the suitcase leaving the bottom half trailing outside the luggage. Then pack a couple sweaters on top of the slacks, folding the pant legs back over the sweaters. Use the same technique to pack skirts and jackets that are longer than your suitcase. Ideally, you will be packing mostly knits and need not worry about wrinkles.

Strap down the contents firmly. Wrinkles form when the clothes are packed loosely enough to shift around inside. You could pad the contents with crumpled plastic dry cleaning bags to help prevent shifting.

Belts can be left long, not rolled, and stretched around the inside circumference of the suitcase. Stagger the buckles so they don't scratch each other.

When packing to come home, you may find that

you've made too many purchases to squeeze everything into your suitcase. This is when you'll be glad if you've brought along a small, expandable tote bag. You could use it as a carry-on bag for your new purchases. Or, if that would make you exceed the two bag carry-on limit, you could stuff it with all your dirty laundry and check it as luggage. If you do check it, make sure it has a luggage tag and lock.

If you must pack any delicate breakables, wrap a T-shirt around them, then place them in the middle layer of your suitcase to keep them well padded by soft clothing.

Off You Go!

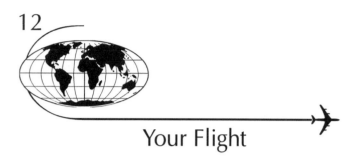

Your Flight

You should really be excited now. You've planned, you've prepared and you've packed. Now, at last, you're really on your way. You're ready for a great vacation, and a wonderful adventure. Congratulations!

Dress comfortably. Knits are perfect because they feel like pajamas but never look like you've slept in them. Go light on makeup, skip the mascara, but go heavy on the moisturizer. Even men should wear a moisturizer when they fly. The dry cabin air can parch our skin.

Give yourself plenty of time to get to the airport. Allow extra time for traffic, parking and long check-in lines, especially if it's the beginning or end of a weekend or holiday. Your airline or travel agent should tell you how early to arrive for your flight.

Check your suitcase, if you brought one. You are normally permitted two pieces of carry-on luggage, plus a purse, umbrella, camera, coat and reading material. Regulations vary by airline, so you might want to ask ahead of time.

For domestic travel, if you already have a boarding card with an assigned seat and no luggage to check, you may proceed straight to your departure gate, clearing security on the way. If you are flying domestic and do have a suitcase to check, you may check it curbside with a porter. Be sure to tip at least a buck a bag. He will put a coded tag on each suitcase checked and staple a matching stub from each tag into your boarding envelope. The tag will have a three letter code for the airport of your destination. Double check to make sure your bag is tagged properly.

For international travel, you must check in at the ticket counter. Normally you must be there two hours prior to departure. You may tip a porter to carry your suitcase to the ticket counter for you, but you must still check it yourself. (Hopefully you haven't packed more than you can handle.) At the ticket counter you'll need to show your passport, visa (if necessary) and ticket. You'll be assigned a seat and given a boarding pass. Give a friendly smile to the agent. Ask very nicely if it would be possible to have an empty seat next to you if the flight isn't too full. If you need leg room, ask for a seat in an emergency exit row. Bulkhead rows also have lots of leg room but mothers with infants are often seated there.

The ticket counter agent will tell you which gate you'll depart from and what time you'll need to be there. In the meantime, you are free to roam the airport, browse the shops (maybe buy a few postcards of your city to show the people you'll meet abroad) or have something to eat or drink.

When you proceed to your gate, you will need to pass through security. For domestic flights, you'll place all of your items on a conveyor belt to pass through the x-ray machine. This normally won't damage film unless you use high speed film, but you may ask to have your film hand inspected. If you're flying to an international destination, you will also be asked a series of questions pertaining to security. It is important that you take this seriously and answer the questions honestly. Did you pack your own luggage? Has the luggage been out of your sight since it was packed? Has anyone given you a gift to take on your trip, or asked you to carry a package for them? Sometimes, for added security, certain items may be confiscated for the duration of the flight. You may be required to hand over batteries from your tape player, liquids and sprays. You'll get these back at your destination. It's a hassle, but, unfortunately, the state of our world makes this all necessary.

The gate area is a good place to relax and check out your fellow passengers. This is a perfect opportunity to meet them and chat with them. Ask the people around you if they have ever been to this destination before. You may meet people who live there and can give you "inside information." Ask what they recommend you see and do, what do the "locals" do for entertainment and what are their favorite restaurants. Ask if they know the hotel you plan to stay at and if it's in a good area. Ask them what native dishes they recommend you try, what do they recommend for evening entertainment and what is the best way to get around town. Perhaps they can expand on what you've already learned from your reading.

When the agents announce the start of boarding, look at the seat number on your boarding card. Families and people needing special assistance will be boarded first, then all other passengers, according to their row numbers, back to front.

When you board, find your seat and stow your carry-on luggage. You may use the overhead compartment or the space under the seat in front of you. Sometimes there are closets for garment bags. Find a pillow and blanket. Even if you don't intend to sleep, you will be more comfortable. Some airplane seats seem to be designed with the body of Quasimodo in mind, so a pillow behind your lower back will give you extra support.

In the spirit of fun, you may ask someone nearby to take a picture of you with your camera as you begin your big adventure. It'll be a great opening shot for your scrapbook.

In the spirit of safety, stand up at your seat and look at all the airplane emergency exits around you. Spot at least two and note that the closest one may be behind you. Now, sit down, fasten your seat belt and look in the seat pocket in front of you for the safety information card. Read it. Finally, on overwater flights, feel under your seat for a small plastic package that contains your life vest. All the information will be repeated during taxi in either a video or a demonstration by your flight attendants. Please pay attention. I don't tell you these things to scare you. I still follow these steps whenever I am a passenger. Think of your knowledge as a free life insurance policy.

During the flight, if you need to sleep (see chapter on Jet Lag) do so as soon as possible!

If you will be awake, then really enjoy your flight. Look out the window, talk to your fellow passengers, ask more questions about your destination. Your flight attendants are usually a great source of information, especially on shopping and eating—two of our favorite pastimes. We are world renowned bargain shoppers. Ask us when we have time, and we will be glad to share our knowledge with you. Flight time is also a great time for reading and writing. You could pore through your travel guides again, or begin recording your thoughts in your journal.

Depending on the length of your flight and the time of day, you may be served a meal or snack. It's best to check in advance, though, because most of the major airlines are cutting back on food services in an effort to cut costs and compete with all the "peanut carriers." It's all to your benefit in lower fares. So, if there's no food service on your flight, why not come prepared with a delicious picnic of your own?

If you drink on the airplane, be aware that alcohol will dehydrate you. It will also pack more of a whollop than you're used to because of the altitude. I won't say don't, just use moderation and also drink plenty of water. Avoid carbonated beverages. Gas expands at high altitudes and you could develop what we flight attendants refer to as "jet belly." It's best to stick with water and juices.

A few words about your friendly flight attendants. People still persist in calling us "stewardesses" even though we prefer the term "flight attendant" which has been in use for over twenty years now—ever since men joined our ranks. The government requires us to be on your flight for your safety, fully trained for emergencies and first aid. Happily, air travel is so safe we rarely need to use this training. So you will see us serving drinks and food, doing our best to keep everyone happy. It's not always easy!

Prior to landing in another country, you will be given a declaration card to fill out with your name, address, passport number and some information about your trip. Complete this before landing and keep it with your passport to show officials when you pass through customs. It's time to be alert now and begin thinking about your arrival. Before you leave the plane, check around your seat to be sure you have all your belongings.

Jet Lag

The goal here is to get your body into synchronization with your new surroundings as quickly as possible. You want to be awake and alert during the day and to sleep soundly through the night. Your body may want to do just the opposite, depending on how far you have traveled east or west. There are things you can do to help your body adjust more quickly and things you can do which will only prolong the agony. I'm going to give you the benefit of my twenty-six years of trial and error.

Scientific studies have been conducted on how to combat jet lag. I've never tried them because they seem like too much trouble. They involve things like fasting, eating at odd times, carbohydrate-loading, and exposure to bright light only at certain times. Let's not make the "cure" worse than the "disease."

Let's just do what it takes to help our body sleep when it should and stay awake when it's supposed to.

Let me first give you an example, from personal experience, of what not to do. At the age of twenty-one I took my first trip to Europe with my dear friend, Linda, who was my roommate at the time. We flew from Chicago to New York, then nonstop to Rome. This being our first flight to Europe, we didn't want to miss a thing; first the beverage service, then the meal, and, later, the movie. We were more than halfway to Rome when the movie ended, then we dozed in the dark like the rest of the passengers. Our nap was cut short when the attendants turned on the cabin lights to serve us breakfast and distribute immigration forms. We'd had, at most, an hour nap. We were zombies. When we got to our hotel, it was morning in Rome and the town was bustling. But there were those beds in our room and, to us, they looked like the sweetest place on earth! The urge was irresistible and we slept until early afternoon. Our mistake in doing so was to keep our poor confused bodies on Chicago time, which means that we were unable to sleep that night, and couldn't help but sleep most of the following day. It was a tough cycle to break. It took us over a week to feel normal, but I learned my lesson.

Let's assume for our example that you are flying from Atlanta to Paris. You'll be departing Atlanta at 7 P.M. and arriving in Paris around 9 A.M. the next day. The problem results from the six hour time change. That 9 A.M. in Paris actually feels like 3 A.M. to your poor body. By the time you check in at your hotel it will be almost 11 A.M. with the Paris day in full swing. I hope you learn from my bad example and do just the opposite: Sleep on the plane the entire flight and stay awake all day when you arrive at your destination. Luckily, from Atlanta, you've got about an eight hour flight to work with. From New York you'd shave about an hour from the flight time. You won't be able to sleep every minute of the flight, but do the best you can; even if you don't sleep soundly the whole time, keep your eyes closed, breathe deeply and relax as best you can.

Your preparation should begin the morning of your flight. If you can get up a bit earlier than usual, it may help you sleep better on the flight. If you are normally a caffeine drinker, cut your intake in half, and do not have any caffeine after 10 A.M. that day. Drink plenty of water all day long to hydrate your body. (There is no humidity on airplanes and the dryness is very uncomfortable on long flights.) Avoid all carbonated beverages. Eat your normal meals for the day, including fresh fruits and vegetables and avoiding greasy foods. Do you have time to eat dinner before heading for the airport? If not, then eat a light meal at the airport after you check in, but before your flight. Keep it as nutritious as possible. Next, I suggest breaking a "scientific" rule and having a glass of wine before your flight. Wine dehydrates you, which is bad, but it relaxes you and will help you sleep, which is good. So have your wine (just one glass), drink some extra water and get on the plane. (If you can't, shouldn't, or don't want to drink alcohol, then of course just skip this step.) Some people suggest using a sleeping pill for the flight, but I don't recommend that for two reasons. In the unlikely case of any emergency, you would be unable to react. And, most likely, it will leave you feeling groggy when you land.

Set your watch to the time at your destination. This is a psychological ploy, but very effective. From this point on, forget about "your" time. Your time now is the new time you've just set on your watch, about 1 A.M. See, doesn't that make you feel more sleepy than if your watch read 7 P.M.? All the good people of Paris are asleep now, and you should be, too.

Smile at the flight attendants and say hello! See if you can figure out who's working your section and politely inform them that you intend to sleep the entire flight and to please not wake you until breakfast. If the plane is not very full, see if you are lucky enough to find a completely empty row (wait till they're finished boarding). If so, lie down on it—the armrests usually can be flipped back. If not, find as much space as you can, make yourself as comfortable as possible, and go to sleep. Always keep a seat belt fastened around your waist, even if you are lying down, just in case of sudden rough air.

Use whatever you need to help you sleep: pillow, blanket, eyeshades, socks to wear instead of your shoes, earplugs or maybe your walkman with a relaxation tape. Many experienced travelers use inflatable pillows. Horseshoe shaped, they fit around your neck and allow you to flop your head to one side or the other without getting a stiff neck—a must when you have to sleep sitting up.

Even if you do not fall into a deep sleep, keep your eyes closed and relax. Your object is to give your body as much rest as possible on the flight. Take small breaks only to drink water, mist your face with your water spray, or use the lavatory (don't forget to put your shoes on). Do not give in to the temptation to eat the meal or watch the movie. Nothing is more important right now than your sleep. Because the flight time is so long, the flight attendants are in no rush to complete the services. The initial beverage service alone might take up more than the first hour of your flight. Then the meal, more beverages, the "duty free" sales and the movie. These services eat up your precious sleep time, so just resist them and console yourself that you can enjoy them all on the flight back.

The more you rest on the flight, the easier it will be for you to stay awake your first day in Europe. If you are lucky, you will get at least five hours of sleep/rest. This will be enough to get you through your first day.

When you are awakened for breakfast, drink some more water and mist your face. You'll be happy if you've brought some "natural tears" type drops to soothe your eyes. Drink some caffeine (coffee or tea) with your meal. This will signal to your body that it's time to wake up.

The airplane lavs will not be looking or smelling their best at this point, but do your best to freshen up. Brush your teeth, splash some water on your face, and freshen your deodorant, if necessary. Then go back to your seat if you need to freshen your makeup, because there's probably a long line for the lav. (I wear very little makeup for these long flights, just plenty of moisturizer. I put on a little makeup before landing.) You will not feel your perkiest, but you will feel a lot better than everyone else on the plane.

You must stay awake your entire first day. Do not take a nap. When you get to your room, unpack, shower, put on fresh clothes, then get out of your room! Fresh air will invigorate you. Stay outdoors as much as possible. Walk in a park, sit at a sidewalk cafe, take a short tour to orient yourself to your new surroundings. Go easy on yourself this first day. Do not plan anything too challenging. Stop and have a cup of coffee when necessary, but do not drink any caffeine after, say, 2 P.M. so you will be able to sleep well that first night. Your goal this first day is to stay awake until 10 P.M.

Toward that end, at 9:30 P.M., you may take one mild, over-the-counter sleeping pill. I do not like to advocate the use of sleeping pills and I only recommend one this first night. But without it, you will probably wake up around 4 A.M. and be unable to go back to sleep. That would only prolong your jet lag. Many flight attendants I know swear by Excedrin PM and they sometimes take one on short layovers when there's not enough time to unwind and barely enough time to get seven hours of sleep. I suggest that you ask your pharmacist to recommend something mild that won't leave you feeling groggy or hung-over in the morning. Perhaps you could do as I do and just take half the dose, or try melatonin instead of a sleeping pill. Please consult with your personal physician before taking either of these medications to make sure they are safe for you and that they do not interfere with any other medication you normally take.

Your body will want to sleep late, but it will be best for you if you're up by 9 A.M. the next morning. Have some coffee or tea to again signal to your body that it is time to be awake.

Even if you follow all of my advice, you will still have a mild case of jet lag. Sorry. There's just no way to totally avoid it except to stay home. But I promise my ideas will lessen your discomfort and you'll feel normal by day three. In the meantime, you will have short, mild periods of feeling tired, sleepy, confused, disoriented and dizzy. These feelings will just wash over you from time to time, especially that first day, then they will pass and you'll feel fine. When they hit, just get some fresh air and breathe deeply. Take a stroll, or just sit down and have a cup of coffee. This is a wonderful way to get into sync with the European cafe life, to try their special coffees and to observe the passing parade of people.

For your return flight to the USA, you'll depart Paris at 11:35 A.M. and arrive in Atlanta at 3:25 P.M. that same day. This time you can stay awake and enjoy every minute! Eat the meal, watch the movie, write in your journal, talk to people.

When you get home, your goal again is to stay awake until 10 P.M. local time. At 9:30 P.M. you may take another of your mild sleeping pills or melatonin to make sure you sleep through the night. Force yourself to get up no later than 9 A.M. the next morning. Sound familiar? From here on, you get over jet lag at home the same way you got over it in Europe.

Jet lag is not a big issue going north or south, and it is not severe with domestic travel where you'll cross no more than three time zones.

Just remember to do what you need to do in order to sleep at night and stay awake during the day. Set your watch to the time of your destination at the beginning of your flight. If it is time to be asleep, sleep. If it is time to be awake, stay awake.

Melatonin

I began researching Melatonin because I'd heard so much about it being used to combat jet lag. My health food store guru told me that it is primarily used as a sleep aid. He said his store can hardly keep up with the demand for it. One customer was cured of a fifteen year case of insomnia. In further reading it occurred to me that melatonin seems to be the "vitamin C" of the 90s. Some studies have shown it to offer many exciting benefits. Among them are not only help in fighting jet lag and insomnia, but also help in the fight against aging and cancer. It seems to boost the body's immune system and protects cells from free-radical damage.

What is melatonin? It is a hormone that occurs naturally in the human body. Secreted by the pineal gland in response to light, melatonin helps regulate the rhythms of our sleep and the action of other hormones. The level of melatonin in our bodies peaks in childhood and continues to decline as we age. Therefore, replacing the older body's "lost" melatonin helps us to "sleep like a baby."

Be cautious with this, as with many other supplements, as the jury is still out over long term effects. Still, as a sleep aid, it seems to me to be more natural and safer than sleeping pills. The pills I have are sublingual (to be dissolved under the tongue) and in 2.5 milligram strength. I usually break the tablet into half dose size. I have always slept well, but I do notice that I drift off to sleep a bit more quickly with melatonin, and I wake up with no groggy after-effect.

The recommended nightly dosage in combating jet lag is 5 milligrams. You should not continue this high a dosage after your jet lag passes. Definitely do not take melatoin combined with a sleeping pill. Read the label carefully for any possible warnings. Melatonin is not to be taken by children, teenagers, pregnant or lactating women, nor by people with certain medical conditions. It is best to ask your doctor about it.

For further information, you may read the articles in *Newsweek,* August 7, l995 and *Newsweek,* November 6, l995. Books include *The Melatonin Miracle,* by Walter Pierpaoli and William Regelson with Carol Colman (Simon & Schuster, $21), *Melatonin: Your Body's Natural Wonder Drug* by Russel J. Reiter and Jo Robinson (Bantam Books, $22.95), *Melatonin: The Anti-Aging Hormone* by Suzanne LeVert (Avon Books, $5.99), *Melatonin: Nature's Sleeping Pill* by Ray Sahelian (Be Happier Press, $13.95) and *Travelers' Health: How to Stay Healthy All Over The World,* by Dr. Richard Dawood (Random House, $18)

Arrival

You've Arrived!

This is when many people enter the "twilight zone." They're in a strange, new place and they get sensory overload because there's noise, confusion and just too much to see all at once. But not you, courageous traveler! Just look for the signs. Every airport has signs that are easy to follow, with pictures as well as words, usually posted around ceiling level. Assuming you have checked a suitcase, first look for a sign with a picture of a suitcase on it and follow the arrow to baggage claim.

If you have landed in another country, you must clear immigration on your way to baggage claim. Make sure you get in the correct line. There will be lines for nationals and other lines for foreigners. You are the foreigner here. Simply show the official your passport and the immigration card that you filled out on the plane. He will keep the card, stamp your passport and then you'll proceed to baggage claim to get your suitcase. Look for the luggage carousel that has your flight number posted above it.

When you have your suitcase and all your belongings, you must go through customs. There will be two lines (again, just keep reading signs), one for people with goods to declare and the other for people with no goods to declare. Your guidebooks have told you the acceptable amounts of liquor, cigarettes and currency you may bring into the country. If you've not exceeded those limits, then you have "nothing to declare." You will most likely be waved through customs, but if you are asked to open your bags, by all means comply and answer all questions.

Money

After clearing customs, your next step is to change some of your money for local currency. Look for a booth or glassed-in office that says "Bank," "Currency Exchange," "Bureau de Change," or something similar or a sign that has a picture of money. Displayed inside will be a chart showing that day's exchange rates for most of the world's currencies. Look for the American flag on the chart and see what your dollars are worth. You'll see two columns of rates; one is for selling dollars, the other for buying dollars. There's often another column listing the rates for travelers checks. You are selling, and you'll get a better rate selling dollars in the form of travelers checks rather than cash. Be aware that there may be a service charge for the transaction. Usually you can get a better rate of exchange at banks or exchange offices in town, so just cash enough for that day (or more if it is a weekend or holiday and the banks will be closed).

Whenever you cash a travelers check, the cashier will need to see your passport. He will give it back to you with the local currency and a receipt. Step aside and count the money, making sure it adds up to the total on the receipt (I do not expect you will be cheated). You must become familiar with the money as quickly as possible. Count the money again, this time with your pocket calculator in hand. Divide the total amount of local currency you received by the amount of dollars you cashed. This way, you are factoring in the service charge to get your real rate of exchange. The resulting number can be used to figure out what things really cost.

An example: You are in Greece and cash a traveler's check for $20. The official rate of exchange posted is $1.00 = 250 Drachma. But the service charge is 2%. You are actually given 4900 Drachma which, divided by twenty, equals 245 Drachma per dollar, which is your real rate of exchange. So when a cab driver tells you he'll charge 1500 Drachma to drive you into town, you divide by 245 to determine the actual cost in dollars (just over $6). The next time you exchange money, you may get a better rate, so again you will follow the same steps to determine your real rate of exchange. You can shop banks and exchange offices, for the best rates, but always figure in the commission. Occasionally you'll find an office that does not charge commission.

If you carry American Express travelers checks, see if there is a local American Express office because they will give you the best rate of exchange with no commission fees.

Credit cards usually give you the best rates of exchange. Your bill will be written in local currency, then will be converted by your credit card company and billed to you in dollars. Charge whatever you can, but many small hotels and shops will not accept credit cards. Many shopkeepers who do accept credit cards will give you a better deal on your purchases if you pay with cash. That is because the credit card company takes a percentage of the merchant's sales that were charged.

For more information about money, credit cards and automated teller machine (ATM) cards, refer to Chapter 8, "Protect Your Belongings."

How to Get From the Airport to Your Hotel

Your guidebooks have probably given you options for getting from the airport to your hotel. There are several choices.

Take a taxi all the way from the airport to your hotel and pray you don't get ripped off. There may be a flat rate charge, or the fare might be strictly meter. There may be an extra charge for luggage, and maybe even an extra charge for the particular time of day you're going. Try to get the driver to quote either a flat rate or an estimate of the meter fare before you get into the cab. I'm very nice to cab drivers and usually offer them some candy and engage them in conversation if they speak any English at all. I hope that they'll like me enough that they won't rip me off, but I also like to find out more about their city from them. If your driver seems nice, friendly and competent I suggest you get his card so you can call him again.

Your other option is public transportation. Most major cities have bus or train service from the airport to a central location in the city. From there you can take a taxi to your hotel. This is much cheaper than taking a taxi the entire distance. Again, look for signs in the airport indicating ground transportation (usually a picture of a bus), or look for an information counter.

Most major cities in the United States have a third option: a bus or van that will pick up many passengers and drop each one at their hotel. It takes a bit longer than a taxi because of the additional stops, but costs much less.

15

Accommodations

Your Hotel

I try to budget for hotels at a rate of $50 per night. In some countries I can get by very nicely for much less, and in others I may have to spend a bit more. In Maui, I knew I would be in my room or on my balcony a great deal of the time writing this book, so I splurged on an ocean view. Normally, my priorities are cleanliness and a safe location that is hopefully central. I usually try for a private bath. I do not care at all about amenities. Your own budget and priorities may differ from mine.

In the United States we have many chains of "budget" hotels that may charge from $27 to $55 per night. Even at those low prices we have certain expectations: A double bed, carpeting, a table and chair, a chest of drawers as well as a closet for our clothes, a television and a telephone. These things are standard here, even in budget hotels.

Overseas? An entirely different story! I could probably devote another book to descriptions of funky little rooms I've stayed in.

In Milan, my room had a bathroom that was added probably a century after the hotel was built. The bathroom was no larger than an airplane lav. The sink was directly above the toilet, and the shower nozzle was in the middle of the ceiling. The floor was slatted with a drain underneath. The bellman showed me that both the sink and the toilet were hinged at the back and could each be latched up against the wall. So, if I needed to use the toilet, I could latch up the sink, and vice-versa. To shower, of course, I'd latch up everything. I started laughing so hard tears were rolling down my cheeks; the bellman laughed, too. Even though we didn't share the same language, I think we both felt that this was just the silliest, most awful, yet ingenious thing we could imagine.

I'm accustomed to not having closets in most old European hotels. Usually there is an armoire instead. But one room I had in Paris offered only a few hooks mounted on the wall. The window curtain matched the bedspread because the window curtain was a bedspread—brown chenille.

My room in Venice was so narrow that I could touch opposite walls at the same time just by stretching my arms. The bed was no wider than a cot.

My bathtub in Lyon was only three feet long, with one half deeper than the other; like an underwater chair.

I have photos at home of all these oddities and I have always been amused by the absurdities I encounter. If you stretch your travel dollar as I do, you'll need quite a sense of humor when you travel overseas. Remember, the less your room costs, the longer you can afford to stay. Be prepared for many differences. Keep in mind that your hotel may be older than our country. To me, this alone is exciting enough to compensate for the lack of convenience. Your room will probably have no television or radio. There may not be a dresser. Your mattress may be older than you are. Your pillow may feel like a slab of concrete. Your towels may be thin and scratchy, and don't expect to see a washcloth. Keep in mind that these are not "chain" hotels, but small, family-owned operations. Each has its own personality; some are delightfully charming. I simply warn you to keep an open mind.

You may certainly ask to see your room before you register. Sometimes there's a world of difference between rooms in the same hotel, so if you don't like the first one, you might ask to see another. If you like the room but it's a bit outside your budget, you could try to negotiate. Perhaps you could get a better price if you stayed longer or if you paid in cash. (It is easier to negotiate in the "off" or "shoulder" seasons than it is in the height of tourist season.) If you think you could do better elsewhere, then politely explain that you would like to check around a bit more. Be careful not to burn any bridges in case you need to come back. Do all negotiating in a spirit of friendliness as opposed to aggression. You do not want to insult or offend your hosts and you'll want to rely a great deal on their kindness during your stay.

When you register, the desk clerk will need to see your passport. This is normal. Sometimes they'll just copy the information they need and hand it back. Sometimes they like to keep it a little longer. Sometimes local regulations require hotels to hold your passport overnight. I have no idea why they need it—perhaps to make sure you're not on some "wanted" list. Just remember to get it back.

If I'll be staying in a room for two nights or more, I prefer to completely unpack. I arrange my things conveniently and make it "home." I'll even buy flowers if I'll be there for awhile. For my Maui vacation I even brought candles. I do not like changing hotels every night. I'd much rather base myself in one place, taking side trips, but getting to know the area I'm in. That way, I don't feel like I'm living out of a suitcase, my hotel staff feels like family and I get a good sense of the location and the people.

It would be nice to learn the name of the desk clerk and ask him or her to teach you how to say a few words in their language—at least "Please," "Thank you," "Good day," and "Good bye." They will be flattered and impressed that you care enough to learn. You may even find that you've made a lifelong friend!

I still correspond with Didier, a young man I met many years ago when he was a bellman in a small Paris hotel. He is now the manager of a fine hotel in the Loire Valley. Through the years I've enjoyed hearing about his marriage to Danielle and the births of their three beautiful children. I treasure his friendship and was fortunate to be able to meet his family on a later trip through the Loire.

Alternative Accommodations

Bed and Breakfasts, or B&Bs for short, can be found throughout the United States, Canada and much of Western Europe. Slightly less expensive than most hotels, they are usually more charming and intimate, offering you a chance to stay in someone's home. You will have a room of your own, either with a private or a shared bathroom. If you are unaccustomed to traveling alone, you may especially enjoy the sense of "home" you will feel in a B&B. The price of your room includes a full breakfast, usually seated at a large table with the other guests. It is fun to sit and chat with other travelers as you start your day. Your hosts will make you feel welcome, usually offering information on things to see and do in the area. For information on B&Bs, write to the tourist information office for your destination. Your guidebooks may also mention some. You can buy books that list and rate B&Bs. Check your travel bookstore or call 800-282-3963 for a copy of the Adventurous Traveler Bookstore catalog which sells, among many other books, Bed and Breakfast guidebooks for many countries.

Homestays is a broad category whose boundary blurs a bit with that of Bed and Breakfasts. You rent a room in someone's home. You will receive your own key and come and go as you please, with care not to disturb anyone. You may or may not have a private bathroom. You may share living quarters with your host family, or you may have your own private entrance. Meals are not normally included unless, for some reason you'd like to negotiate that with your host. You can find out about homestays through tourist agencies or book them through accommodation agencies that can be found in airports, in train stations and often at a central location in the city. Check your guidebooks for homestay information particular to your destination. Often people with rooms to rent will stand in the arrival area of airports and train stations holding signs. Sometimes you can walk around town and see signs in the windows of some homes offering rooms to rent. Homestays are cheaper than Bed and Breakfasts, and usually less charming; but they do give you an authentic peek into the homes and home life of the "natives."

Youth Hostels — not just for kids anymore, though certainly youth prevails. I confess I have never stayed in a youth hostel, but I did pop into one recently when I was in Vancouver. The friendly young woman at the front desk gave me a tour. The place was Spartan but clean with a large kitchen for the guests to use, and separate shower and sleeping facilities for men and women. The sleeping rooms were filled with bunk beds and lockers for storing belongings. There were a couple small rooms, each with a double bed and a bunk bed, but these are reserved for families. Travelers either bring their own sheetsack (made by folding a flat sheet in half and sewing up the bottom and side edge), pillowcase and towels or rent linens from the hostel. If your privacy is less important than your budget, then by all means, give this a try. It certainly would be a great way to meet other travelers.

The annual hostel membership fee of $25 entitles you to reserve a bunk in any of five thousand hostels in seventy countries for the rate of just a few dollars a night. Membership also entitles you to discounts on such things as transportation, car rentals, restaurants and museum admissions. For more information and an application, contact HI-AYH (Hosteling International-American Youth Hostels), 733 15th St., NW, Suite 840, P.O. Box 37613, Washington, DC 20013-7613. (202)783-6161, or Fax (202)783-6171.

Phone Calls

Be careful about making phone calls from your hotel. Almost all hotels now charge a fee, even for local calls. Long distance calls may be billed at a much higher rate with the hotel keeping the profit. You may check with the desk clerk about your hotel's policy or just play it safe and use public phones using an international calling service such as AT&T "USA Direct."

Another phoning option is to buy prepaid calling cards. Many countries have introduced these. You buy them at the post office and may use them in specially adapted phones. The card is worth a set amount, say $10 or $20, depending on how much you paid for it. You insert the card into the adapted phone, make your call and the amount used for your call is automatically deducted from the value of the card. Of course more is deducted for long distance than for local calls. When I use these cards to phone overseas, I warn the person I'm calling that we will be cut off when the value of the card runs out.

Still another way to phone home from overseas is from the post office. Check your guidebooks or with your hotel staff for the location of the post office with long-distance phone service. You go there and use their designated phones to dial direct, usually from a private booth. Then you pay the post office clerk for the price of your call. You will pay the normal long distance fee with no added service charge. Sometimes you will wait in line with many other budget travelers—another opportunity to make friends and swap stories.

16

Eating and Drinking

Many people are uncomfortable about eating alone. But it can be a learned pleasure. An hour or two alone in a restaurant gives us welcome time to set down our bag, get off our feet and relax. We can reflect on our experiences, make plans, or just let our minds go blissfully blank. Use the time as you please, whether to think, write in your journal, write a few postcards, make notes to yourself, read a bit in your guidebook, study a map or simply sit back in your chair enjoying the good food, a glass of wine and the luxury of being waited on. It is a great time to people-watch, notice details, perhaps smile and exchange pleasantries with the wait staff and people seated nearby.

I welcome the air of mystery that surrounds a woman dining alone. Not that I cause a stir—you needn't worry about jaws slacking and conversation coming to a standstill as you enter the room alone. It's just that there seems to be a natural curiosity of a friendly sort that does not make me the least bit uncomfortable. Waiters see my journal and often ask if I'm a writer. In some countries, if you seem receptive, people at nearby tables may initiate conversation. In others, such as England, France, and most northern European countries, privacy is sacred and yours will not be intruded upon—you will have to make the first move.

To make dining alone a pleasure, take care to choose an appropriate restaurant. Sometimes it won't matter so much. When you're simply hungry or hurried, any old place will do. But, usually, for a leisurely meal, it's nice to walk around checking out many restaurants before you decide which one to enter. You can look at the menus posted outside the doors to see what you might select and to compare prices. Look at the interior of the restaurant— is it clean, peaceful, attractive? Are they playing soft jazz or classical music in the background? Flowers, candles or soft lighting make it further appealing.

I personally prefer small, quiet places where the waiter won't be too rushed to be attentive and may even have time to chat as he serves me. At times, though, the other end of the spectrum is fun. I remember a tiny place in Buenos Aires that was decidedly not attractive—two-tone green painted walls, bright lighting and small wooden tables with mis-matched chairs all jumbled close together. The attraction was food—good, plentiful and cheap. The place was bustling with friendly locals.

My friend, Alice, will test a place by first sitting down for a cup of coffee or glass of wine. Then, if she feels comfortable, she will stay and order a meal. When asked if she had a secret to overcoming her fear of dining alone, she smiled and answered, "Breathe!"

The more experience you have eating alone, the more comfortable it will become. So it will help you to practice in your own town prior to your travels. Solicit restaurant recommendations from your friends or find places on your own where you feel comfortable—and I don't mean fast food places! Take a book or journal if you must for security, but try putting them away for awhile as you gain confidence. Learn to "breathe," relax and enjoy! Luxuriate in the experience of quiet time to yourself with good food and the chance to be waited on.

Another approach is to make lunch your main meal of the day. Many people eat lunch alone, so perhaps you won't feel so odd. Then you can graze your way through the dinner hour, stopping for a sandwich, soup, or just munching an apple as you stroll.

You've heard the saying, "When in Rome, do as the Romans do." When I travel I especially enjoy eating and drinking as the natives do. It's a great way to immerse yourself in another culture. It will usually save you money, too. We've all heard horror stories about the cost of eating a hamburger in Tokyo. But why pay so much money to eat what is boringly common in our own country when we can try a more typical Japanese meal of noodles in a tasty broth with bits of fish or meat and vegetables for a fraction of the cost? Normally I am a wine drinker, but in Thailand wine is very expensive because it is all imported. Yet the Thais brew their delicious Singha beer which is a perfect accompaniment to their flavorful food and much cheaper to drink than wine would be. It is always less expensive to eat and drink locally produced food and beverages, and so much more fun!

People are always flattered and happy to help you when you show an interest in their cuisine. Ask the locals that you meet to recommend their favorite restaurants. Lyon is the gastronomic capital of France. The restaurants are excellent but most are quite pricey and beyond my budget. The kindly desk clerk at my hotel gave me the names of two restaurants that he frequents and marked them on my map for me. They were not at all fancy, but served delicious hearty food at very reasonable prices. Ask people you meet to tell you about their favorite dishes and to write down the names for you. George, who owns the Blazar Bar in Santorini recommended his favorite appetizer, tsatsiki, made with yogurt, cucumber and lots of garlic. It's mouth-watering spread on thick, chewy slices of Greek bread.

I hope that you will foster a spirit of adventure and be willing to try new things. I have gotten more adventurous over the years, but I remember well that first trip to Europe with my friend Linda. We went to a Roman restaurant around six o'clock in the evening. We were starving, but of course the Romans eat much later so we were the first and only ones there. The waiters were kind, attentive, and I'm sure very much amused by us. I can't remember what we ate, but I do remember that they brought us a fresh fruit tray for dessert from which we selected oranges. We cut into the oranges and were just horrified at what we saw. They were very dark and red inside. I guess we thought they were diseased or something and we were debating what to do when the waiter explained to us that these were nice, normal "blood oranges," and quite delicious! On that same trip, in Athens, we followed a recommendation from our guidebook of a restaurant which served a twenty-one course seafood meal. One course was clams on the half shell. The guidebook cautioned us to drip lemon juice on each clam to determine its freshness, yet when each fresh clam actually squirmed in reaction to the acid, we simply could not eat them! Another course was octopus, which I tasted, but only after making Linda cut off all the suction cups on the tentacles.

Now, twenty-six years later, I am willing to at least taste almost everything, including "prairie oysters" (bull testicles—quite tasty) in Argentina, jellyfish tentacles in Korea (tasteless, and felt like a mouthful of cellophane tape), grilled octopus in Greece (delicious), and pigs feet (too fatty) in Paris. I especially love trying exotic fruits and vegetables. In Hawaii I really enjoyed eating charamoya which is similar to the guanabana I had in Costa Rica—an irregularly shaped green fruit with a sweet, pudding-textured pulp inside and hard black seeds.

Luscious! In Thailand as well as Costa Rica I fell in love with many other foreign fruits. Malaysia has their infamous durian fruit, "tastes like heaven, smells like hell," which people either love or hate—I liked it better on my second try. It's very rich and creamy with a distinctive smell so pungent many hotels will not let you keep one in your room.

I have been a vegetarian for about five years now, but I feel so strongly that food is an important part of a country's culture that, when I travel, I do not restrict myself to a meatless diet, though I do still try to eat lots of fruits, vegetables and breads, especially whole grain breads. I loved the "wheaten" bread of Ireland which was served at breakfast. I lose my sense of adventure about eating only when I feel it might endanger my health. I, for example, declined the opportunity to eat dead waterbugs in Bangkok which were offered to me by an engaging street vendor who urged, "Three baht, you eat!" Curious to see just how they were eaten, I replied, "I'll pay you three baht, you eat!", which he did, showing me that you break it open in sections, the back end containing eggs, the chest part "like chicken" inside. I later mentioned that experience to one of our pilots who told me, "Oh, we used to eat bowls-full of those bugs while we played cards and drank beer in Viet Nam. We'd wake up the next morning with terrible breath." I should say so.

If language is a problem, you can buy tiny menu dictionaries in several languages; I have versions in French and Spanish. Your guidebook probably has a section on food which will help you. Many "tourist" restaurants have menus printed in different languages. These places can be a relief when you're too frazzled to cope with a dining adventure, but please don't make a habit of them. Try to find a charming restaurant that is not overrun by tourists. Have in mind the type of meal you want (chicken, for example, or soup with salad) and let your waiter help you from there. Or ask your waiter to recommend something for you. You can also notice what other people are having and ask to have the same. Many restaurant people speak at least a little English, but if language is a problem, don't be afraid to point or even draw a picture of what you want. In Greece, sometimes the waiter will simply take you into the kitchen and let you choose your meal!

If you love to eat "fast food" you can rest assured that the golden arches and the colonel have preceded us almost every place on earth. But shame on you if you eat there! Why travel all that distance to eat "American"? Be brave and try the local fast food instead. In Prague you can buy hot sausages served in a bun. Paris has its own version of a hot dog—served on French bread with mustard so spicy it will clear your sinuses. Paris also has crepe stands. You chose the filling—anything from cheese to Grand Marnier—and it's made while you watch. Croque Monsieur, a toasted ham and cheese sandwich, is another French favorite. My favorite snack in Greece is the souvlaki pita, bits of grilled meat along with french fries, onion, a yogurt sauce and seasoning pepper all rolled up in a pita bread. Get the idea? You can enjoy a tasty, quick and inexpensive meal while still learning more about the local eating customs.

Continental breakfasts vary a bit from country to country, but standard is coffee and some kind of bread with jam. Some countries will add a little cheese. In France, hot chocolate is another beverage choice and the bread includes those fabulous buttery croissants.

Local beverages are a treat to sample. Almost every country produces some specialty in the way of beer, wine or distilled spirits. These are fun to try, as are the aperitifs and after dinner drinks. Each country has its own style of coffee, too: Cafe au Lait, Cappuccino, Espresso, Turkish coffee, Thai iced coffee, Greek iced coffee and on and on. I love coffee and it's fun to try all the different styles. Be aware that if you want a second cup of coffee overseas, you are expected to pay for it, as there are no free refills. But their coffee is much richer that ours, so I doubt you'll need more.

In Kuala Lumpur I drank iced te tarik, tea which is brewed strong then poured back and forth with great flourish between two cups held at least three feet apart. It was mixed with condensed milk and served to me, not in a cup, but in a plastic bag with a handle attached and a straw. I took pictures as I watched it being made for me. Also in Kuala Lumpur, I tried a drink which was quite good made from soy milk and sweetened with syrup. When you sit at sidewalk cafes, notice what other people are drinking. If you see something interesting, ask your waiter what it is. Learn about fun beverages like soda water mixed with colorful flavored syrups, or Italy's Orangina, a refreshing soft drink that's not too sweet. Coca Cola is everywhere, but why not try something that you can't find at home?

Be aware that most cultures use little or no ice in their cold drinks. The excessive cold is thought to impair digestion, harm the teeth and distort the flavor of the beverage. You'll note other differences as well. Butter is seldom served with bread and ketchup is seldom served with anything. Be a good sport and just try things their way.

Ice cream, gelatto and shaved ice desserts are wonderful to try in the countries you visit. I'm especially fond of hazelnut gelatto. In Kuala Lumpur I ate a treat that is called "ABC" for short. I saw someone eating it in a food court at the Central Market and asked him what it was. He gave me a Malay word which I couldn't grasp, so he said "Just ask for 'ABC'" and pointed the way to the vendor. It's a dessert served in a bowl and is made of a mound of shaved ice, brown syrup, red syrup, green pandan noodles, corn (yes, corn), and tiny red beans. It was unusual, colorful, good and refreshing.

Often I'll take pictures of my meals. Sometimes a meal is so beautiful, unusual, or delicious looking that I just want to "save" it in a photo. These photos bring back tasty memories and are fun to show to friends.

Most restaurants in our country will bring you the check when you've finished eating or drinking. Then you are expected to leave. Not so overseas. You may linger for hours at a European sidewalk cafe. It's like having a front row seat at the theater of life!

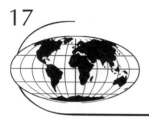

17

Culture Gap

*"Toto, I've a feeling we're not
in Kansas anymore."*

DOROTHY, IN *"THE WIZARD OF OZ"*

There are culture gaps even between neighborhoods within our own cities; differences dictated by race, ethnic background, religion and relative wealth or poverty. Perhaps we can think of culture gaps on our own street, in our own apartment building, and, especially if we have teenagers, even in our own home. We bridge these gaps by getting to know one another and striving to understand the underlying reasons for the differences. The same applies when we travel.

I believe that travel, particularly this kind of solo, one-on-one travel, shows us that, in all the important ways, people the world over are basically the same.

Science is reaching a similar conclusion. In their book, *Shadows of Forgotten Ancestors*, Carl Sagan and Ann Druyan explain that every person in the world shares 99.9 percent of the same DNA sequences, "All humans, no matter how ethnically diverse, are essentially identical." They write, "Of the immense number of possible beings, realized and unrealized, we are all cut from the same cloth, made on the same pattern, granted the same strengths and weaknesses, and will ultimately share the same fate."

It is, I reckon, the 0.1 percent of difference that keeps life interesting. And it is the cultural differences that make travel endlessly fascinating. The wonder of how people so essentially like us can have such different habits, customs, beliefs and behavior. How we deal with the differences matters.

We're only human and it's among our weaknesses to believe that our way is the right way. We tend to recoil at that which is strange to us. As a "bug-o-phobic," that was certainly my reaction to the dead bugs for sale as food in Bangkok. I've since read that the populations of more than half the countries on Earth routinely eat insects. Intentionally. (Not accidentally, as with the occasional dead gnat inadvertently overlooked on your lettuce leaf.)

I was once caught by a sudden downpour in Paris, so I ducked into the nearest cafe. The rain showed no signs of abating, so I ordered a half carafe of red wine and sat down with my journal for several hours. The cafe was on the Rue St. Honore in a very touristy area. While I sat there the table next to me was filled three times, each time with a different group of tourists from America. Each group had a set of complaints: "My room is small and the furniture is old.", "You can never get ketchup in these restaurants.", "The TV in my room only has one station in English." They all seemed to be longing for things to be just the way they were at home, so what was the point of their travel? They will return home saying they didn't like Paris without ever having troubled themselves to know the place or the people.

The way we react to other cultures is sometimes unconscious. We tend to judge groups according to the standards and values of our own culture. For example, what do you think of someone who avoids direct eye contact? What do you think when someone has a limp handshake? What do you assume when you see two men embrace and kiss? When you see two women walking arm in arm? When you observe children drinking wine? Your assumptions could be right IF we're talking about Americans. But what if we're not?

What's appropriate in one culture may be taboo in another. For example the Japanese believe that a firm handshake is too aggressive, and that direct eye contact is intimidating. Our gesture for "okay" with the circle formed by touching the thumb and index finger is considered obscene in some countries. Same with our "thumbs up" and "V" for victory. Many Asian and Middle East cultures believe that the foot is the lowliest, dirtiest part of the body, therefore it is considered an insult for you to show the bottom of your shoe, as you would if you crossed your legs with one ankle resting on the other knee.

Luckily for unknowing travelers, allowances are made for our ignorance due to the fact that we are new in the area. Nonetheless, it is a wise traveler who cares enough to observe carefully what the natives are doing, asks questions and perhaps does some reading on cultural differences prior to the trip.

Your guidebooks for each specific country will no doubt give you a few tips. There are books you can find which will give you more information. Two that I've found interesting are *Gestures,* by Roger E. Axtell, and *Kiss, Bow, or Shake Hands,* by Terri Morrison, Wayne A. Conaway, and George A. Borden, Ph.D. The former, as you can guess, is all about gestures and body language that are used around the world, and what they mean in each country. The latter is aimed at the business traveler but is very useful for the solo traveler as well, offering lots of cultural information about each country. *Culturgrams* are four-page newsletters offered for each country describing the people, their customs, manners and lifestyles. They also give references for further study. They can be ordered by writing to Publication Services, David M. Kennedy Center for International Studies, 280 HRCB, Brigham Young University, Provo, Utah, 84602.

If you do not speak the language of the country you are in, be a little apologetic about it, especially in France, and at least try to learn a few phrases. After all, you are the foreigner here. It will serve you well to be a bit humble about expecting people there to speak your language. Try not to appear exasperated if you have trouble communicating. Do not speak louder, but rather speak a little more slowly, carefully enunciating each word.

In traveling we must overcome many cultural prejudices and know that ours is only one way of life. There are countless others, each deserving of our respect. Remember that human kindness transcends culture. People the world over respond to sincerity and friendliness.

In each of us there still resides the essence of our child. Travel in the spirit of that child, filled with curiosity and wonder, with an open mind and open heart. Do not judge. Observe, enjoy, participate!

To learn about another culture is to have greater understanding of our own, of our world, and of ourselves. And to make a friend overseas is to build yet another bridge across the culture gap.

18

Explore, Have Fun, Meet People

"There's an undeniable romance to travel. Part of it is knowing that unexpected things are going to happen. If you travel with your eyes open and are willing to talk to people, travel can still be an adventure."

CHARLES KURALT

Any of you who are still skeptical about traveling alone are probably sitting there thinking, "All right, maybe solo travel is easy and safe, but what the heck do I do when I get there and I'm all alone?" Never fear, you're going to get out, explore, have fun and meet lots of people in the process.

You must fight feelings of shyness and fear when they threaten to keep you from happiness. I had those feelings on a short trip I took to a golf and beach resort in Florida. I was recovering from a broken romance and my self-esteem was basement-level. I got to my room, unpacked, then just sat on the edge of the bed feeling alone, scared and sorry for myself. I wrestled those feelings and reckoned how silly it was to stay in my room. I forced myself to walk over to the golf clubhouse and was soon teeing off alone. After a couple holes of play, I caught up to a twosome of retired men who invited me to join them. I was quickly engaged in the easy, joking camaraderie of the game and began to relax and enjoy. Life looked good again. I signed up to play golf every day, played with different people each time and made some friends. That turned out to be a wonderful week!

Traveling alone does not mean being alone. One of the reasons you're going alone is because it's easier to meet people.

On my most recent trip to the Greek Islands, I was "alone" only two out of the seventeen days I was there. By alone, I mean I would spend the entire day in my own company chatting only briefly with shopkeepers, waiters or my hotel staff. "Not alone" would mean that, for at least a short part of the day, I'd have a companion to talk with and maybe sightsee with. Among the people I met on that trip:

• Mary, a neurosurgical nurse from London. Mary and I met on the island of Crete and shared four days exploring two cities together and talking for hours over delicious Greek iced coffee.

• Philip, a university professor from Manchester. We met at an outdoor cafe when I first arrived in the tiny village of Spili. He invited me to come with him in his rental car to see an old fort that afternoon. He was a perfect gentleman and wonderful company. I saw him for a short while each day that we were in Spili, then, on a whim, I accepted his invitation to ride with him to see the city of Chania. I gladly treated him to dinner there in gratitude for his providing the transportation. I have a fond memory of our harmonizing on old songs as we drove through the hills of Crete, "When the red, red robin comes bob, bob bobbin' along, along…"

• John and Maureen, a delightful couple from Vancouver. I met them on the ferry boat from Crete to Santorini and they ended up staying at the same tiny hotel as I. We met each evening on our shared hotel terrace to watch the sunset, drink Greek wine, munch pistachios and other snacks. We talked and laughed for hours. One evening Ofir and Mira, a young couple from Israel who were also at our hotel, told us that the cactus pears growing on the adjacent cliff are a delicious fruit that they enjoy eating at home. So John rigged up a "pear picking device" made from a long stick with an empty can attached. He clambered onto the cliff, while I recorded his adventure on film. Soon we were all enjoying his tasty harvest.

- Theo, a restaurant owner on the island of Paros, who was happy to show me his island in the hours before he had to open his restaurant.
- Manolis, the manager of my Santorini hotel who brought me breakfast every morning on my terrace and showed me how to make Greek-style iced coffee.

There were many others I met and shared bits of my days with; a friendly dinner conversation with a German woman who was sitting alone at the next table, a long chat with a young Greek girl on the ferry boat, pleasant talks with shopkeepers and waiters—many happy moments that made me feel anything but alone.

Where do you start? Right in your hotel. You begin by talking to the staff; this is your family while you are there, your support group. Greet them with a smile, remember their faces and maybe even learn their names. Ask them to help you learn a few phrases in their language. They'll be so flattered that you care enough to try, because most tourists don't bother.

Start exploring slowly your first day. Your jet lag will be like a little fog that comes and goes. Find out about your hotel. Where is breakfast served? Is there a restaurant? A bar? Does your hotel have a tour desk? If not, where is the nearest one?

Explore the neighborhood around your hotel. Walk around the block, down the street. Wander where impulse leads you, noting landmarks on your way. Take the time to get your bearings and feel familiar with your new surroundings.

Stop at a cafe when you need a rest. Consider asking someone to take your picture. My camera has been in the hands of people all over the world who were kind enough to oblige. It's a good way to meet people and, if they are also tourists, you can return the favor.

When you sit in cafes, people-watch. Notice details: clothing, hair, grooming, gestures, attitude. What are people eating and drinking? How are they eating—how do they hold their fork? Their cigarette? Can you spot other tourists? Can you guess what country they are from? Can you spot other Americans? What makes us look different? While you're taking note of all the contrasts, always keep in mind the many ways we're all the same. Record your observations in your journal.

You might take a half-day sightseeing tour your first or second day. This will give you an overview of the city and an idea of places you'll want to return to for a closer, more in-depth look. It will also help you get your bearings and a feel for how large the city is. Many cities have a river flowing through them and a river cruise is a wonderfully relaxing way to tour. A few of these cities are London, Paris, Prague, Amsterdam, Budapest and Bangkok.

Find out what other tours are available. Nightclub tours are great if you are nervous about going out alone at night. There are also all-day tours and even overnight tours to places beyond the city you're in. In San Jose, Costa Rica I booked an all-day tour that took me out into the countryside, to a resort where we got to swim in a stream with a thermal pool and waterfall, then to watch a live volcano. The tour included lunch and several other stops. I met some nice people and had a delightful day.

If you feel more confident and adventurous, read the

tour company's brochures for ideas, then head out on your own using a train or public bus. Any good guidebook should explain how to do this and it will save you a lot of money, too.

Find the local tourist office. Your guidebook should give the location, often near the train station or a major tourist attraction. You can get up-to-date information here on hotels, bed and breakfasts, and things to do including festivals, concerts, theater and sporting events. I relied heavily on tourist offices when I traveled through Yugoslavia. They found me guest rooms for as little as $15 per night. I obtained concert information from the tourist offices in Prague. The staff of the tourist office in Sintra, Portugal was able to direct me to a delightful farmers' market which was just outside of town.

Learn how to take public transportation. Your guide-book should explain this, but check with the people in your hotel as well. They can also tell you if it's safe to use public transportation after dark. It's a great way to mingle with the locals as they go about their daily routine. They will be very helpful in pointing out your correct stop, once they understand you're a tourist. Don't be afraid to ask for help. Public transportation will save you a lot of money over taxis, but more importantly will place you smack in the middle of the culture you've come to observe.

When you meet other tourists, compare notes. Ask them where they've been, what they've seen and done, what they recommend and what else they plan to see. Ask them about their own country as well—you may want to add it to your list of places to visit.

One of my very favorite ways to explore a different culture is to shop in their grocery stores. You'll see many familiar items made by American companies, but you'll also find many unusual and sometimes exotic things as well. You can buy the makings of a wonderful picnic for yourself: fresh fruit, bottled water, yogurt, bread, cookies, cheese, etc. Grocery stores are also a great source for affordable gifts and souvenirs. In England, look for marmalades, preserves, tea and biscuits. In France, check out the mustards (I've found the cheaper, the better, at least for strength), the salad dressings and herbs. In other countries you'll find olives and olive oils, coffee beans, soups, cereals, puddings, spices and seasonings. Browse the aisles for canned goods—curried tuna in Singapore, steak and kidney pie in England, braised octopus in Greece, cassoulet in France. Scan the local wines, juices and soft drinks. Many things you see will catch your eye and spark your curiosity. They will also be a nice reminder of your vacation.

Pharmacies are also fun to browse. Check out the creams, lotions, shampoos, soaps and toothpastes.

Another great way to immerse yourself in the culture is to shop the various markets where people go to buy fresh produce, meat, fish, household supplies, clothing or even antiques. These are usually outdoor events, though sometimes they are under a roof or tent. Each vendor sets up his or her own display. If you don't see prices posted, then bargain away! Your guidebook should mention these markets, but also ask at your hotel. Sometimes they only operate between certain hours and on certain days. Some are centrally located but others are on the outskirts of town. Markets are usually crowded, bustling and picturesque. Purchase something, participate, take lots of pictures! I have wonderful snapshots of different types of markets from all over the world:

- The flea market in Rome where I bought a shirt, a belt and some cassette tapes.
- A small farmers' market in a Slovakian town where people sell produce and flowers. Many of these farmers seemed to be barely scraping by. One poor elderly

woman had only a few root vegetables and a small pile of dried beans to sell.

- The Central Market in San Jose, Costa Rica where I saw many unusual types of fruit including the brightly colored fruit that grow attached to cashew nuts! There were tubs of fish, a pail of sea turtle eggs, leather belts and bags, vegetables. Many vendors were selling assortments of dried plants and herbs, most of which I did not recognize. These, I was told, were for medicinal and other uses including insect repellent.

- In Hong Kong there is the bird market which offers for sale an assortment of birds, intricate bamboo cages, tiny blue and white china bowls for seed as well as a fantastic array of live lizards, worms and insects to feed to the birds.

- The markets in Thailand—the most extraordinary I've seen so far—where carts are piled high with fresh orchids, exotic fruits and vegetables. I also saw dried pig faces for sale and huge dead waterbugs neatly arranged on trays. And those were just the things I could recognize!

- A very large flea market on the outskirts of Paris where I discovered a vendor who sold old postcards—many were over one hundred years old, sent by French travelers to their friends and families back home. I bought some postcards of old Chicago, Detroit and San Francisco. These were fun souvenirs, inexpensive and very easy to pack.

Remember to guard your money at these markets. It's easy to be distracted and pickpockets work these crowds.

I've gotten into the habit of mailing a few postcards to myself while traveling. I write a few cheerful words and a small detail of the day to jog my memory when I receive it. I'll keep the cards on my fridge at home for awhile then add them to my growing collection.

Attend a cultural event such as a ballet, concert or a play if language will not be a problem. In Paris I tried one day to see the inside of the celebrated Opera House with its Chagall ceiling and famous chandelier, but it was closed due to rehearsals in progress. On impulse I bought a ticket for a dance performance that evening. I couldn't figure out the ticketing and paid a price somewhere in the middle range—around $20. To my amazement, the usher led me to a private box just above and to the left of the stage. There were maybe half a dozen seats in the box, but that night it was mine alone! I delighted in watching three performances of modern dance, a new experience for me, and enjoyed shouting "Bravo!" through the applause with the nice French couple seated in the next box. The Chagall, the chandelier and the performance were magnificent.

Make time in your itinerary to get out of the major cities and explore the small towns, villages and countryside. You cannot know England by London alone. Think of it this way. I frequently have on my flights travelers from European countries who are seeing the United States for the first time. I love to ask them what they plan to see while they're here. The reply is always something like, "New York, Miami and Disney World." There are slight variations, sometimes including Washington, DC or Los Angeles. The thing is, you know they are going to be seeing just the major tourist attractions of just the major cities. We all know that, to get a real sense of our country, you must balance the hustle-bustle of the cities with a view of everyday life in the suburbs and small towns. Of course you want to see the main cities, but, while you're there, buy a round-trip train or bus ticket to a nearby small town or two. Spend a day exploring and discovering a different facet of the country you're visiting.

When Chicago, my hometown, is on the itinerary of travelers, I always ask what they plan to see and do in my fine city. Their answers are always, "The Sears Tower, the Museum of Science and Industry, and a Magnificent Mile shopping spree." Usually they plan only a day or two for one of the most culturally and architecturally exciting cities in the world. When travelers are open to my suggestions, I write a lengthy list of things to do and places to go that would give them a truer and more intimate sense of Chicago including where to get the best hot dog, pizza and hamburger. To a group of German tourists, I recommended a small local brewery—casual, friendly and decidedly not touristy. I recommend my favorite restaurants for delicious food at modest prices. Music is a large part of Chicago's culture and I offer names of great places to listen to live jazz and blues. I suggest taking in a sporting event such as baseball at our beautiful old classic, Wrigley Field. I tell them they can get a true glimpse of the city on a walk through Lincoln Park to see Chicagoans out jogging, walking, biking, barbecuing and playing baseball. I also tell them the park has a free zoo and wonderful views of Lake Michigan. Given more than a couple days here, I suggest that travelers stroll through some of our many fascinating ethnic neighborhoods. I recommend that they take a train to nearby small towns like Hinsdale or Naperville, or up to Ravinia in Highland Park for an outdoor classical concert. Do you get the idea? To really know a place, we must go beyond the tourist attractions that are all detailed in our guidebooks. The guidebooks are simply our starting point. We must meet the people who live there and find out from them how to participate in their typical activities.

When you travel alone, strive to participate in the life of the culture to the greatest extent possible. Talk with people. Behave as if you're attending a party. It is the party of life. You are expected to mingle!

Travelers' Code of Ethics

- Travel in a spirit of humility and with a genuine desire to meet local people.

- Be sensitive to the feelings of local people and try to avoid offensive behavior, particularly when taking photographs.

- Cultivate the habit of listening and observing, rather than merely hearing or seeing.

- Realize that other people may have concepts of time and other thought patterns that are very different—not inferior—only different.

- Instead of seeing only the "beach paradise," discover the richness of another culture and way of life.

- Get acquainted with local customs and respect them.

- Cultivate the habit of asking questions instead of knowing all the answers.

- Remember that you are only one among many visitors; do not expect special privileges.

- Bargain sensitively. Realize that the "deal" you obtain is only possible because of the low wages paid to the maker.

- Make no promises to local people that you cannot fulfill.

- Reflect daily on your experiences and try to deepen your understanding.

- Think about your interactions with other cultures and environments. Avoid enriching your experience at the expense of your host country or its people.

The travelers' code of ethics was developed in 1975 by the Christian Conference of Asia and is published in the Single-Friendly Travel Directory by Connecting newsletter.

Happy Trails to You!

Now, traveler, it's time to follow your dream. Let nothing deter you. When our old friend fear appears and you hear that babbling voice in your head saying, "What are you, crazy? You can't do that!", tell that voice to just watch and you'll show it what you can do!

Wander, and know that you already have friends all over the planet. You just haven't met them yet. Wherever you go, guides and helpers will be there when you need them. And you will find strength you never knew you had.

As our world grows smaller, we must strive to put a human face on it. We're all on this same spaceship, Earth, cruising to the same ultimate fate. Let's get to know one another and make it a meaningful journey.

Foreign Tourist Offices

You may call or write to the following tourist agencies for information on the countries they represent. They may be able to provide you with maps, brochures and information on hotels, transportation, climate, national holidays, special events, shopping and more. The information in this section is accurate at the time of publication, but is subject to change.

Argentina Tourist Information
P.O. Box 1758
Madison Square Station
New York, NY 10159-1758
212-765-8833
or 800-722-5737

Aruba Tourism Authority
1000 Harbor Blvd.
Weehawken, NJ 07087
800-862-7822

Australian Tourist Commission
847-296-4900

Austrian National Tourist Board
P.O. Box 1142
New York, NY 10108-1142
212-944-6880

Austrian National Tourist Office
500 N. Michigan Ave. #1950
Chicago, IL 60611
312-644-8029

Bahamas Tourist Office
150 East 52nd St.
New York, NY 10022
212-758-2777

Bahamas Tourist Office
3450 Wilshire Blvd. #208
Los Angeles, CA 90010
213-385-0033

Bahamas Tourist Office
8600 W. Bryn Mawr Ave. #820N
Chicago, IL 60631
773-693-1111
or 800-422-4262

Barbados Board of Tourism
800 Second Ave.
New York, NY 10017
212-986-6516
or 800-221-9831

Barbados Board of Tourism
3440 Wilshire Blvd. #1215
Los Angeles, CA 90010
213-380-2198

Belgian Tourist Office
780 Third Ave.
New York, NY 10151
212-758-8130

Belize Tourist Board
421 Seventh Ave. #1110
New York, NY 10001
212-563-6011

Bermuda Department of Tourism
310 Madison Ave.
New York, NY 10017
800-223-6106

Bermuda Department of Tourism
150 N. Wacker Dr. #1070
Chicago, IL 60606
312-782-5486

Bolivian Tourist Information Office
3014 Massachusetts Ave. NW
Washington, DC 20008
202-483-4410 (x23)

Brazilian Tourism Foundation
1050 Edison St. #C2
Santa Ynez, CA 93460
800-544-5503

British Tourist Authority
625 N. Michigan Ave. #1510
Chicago, IL 60611
800-462-2748

British Tourist Office
551 Fifth Ave.
New York, NY 10176
212-986-2200

Canadian Tourist Office:
888-447-4404

Each province has their own tourism division

Alberta
800-661-8888

British Columbia
800-663-6000

Manitoba
800-665-0040

New Brunswick
800-561-0123

Newfoundland & Labrador
800-563-6353

Northwest Territories
800-661-0788

Nova Scotia
800-565-0000

Ontario
800-ONTARIO

Prince Edward Island
800-463-4734

Quebec
800-363-7777

Saskatchewan
800-667-7191

Yukon
800-789-8566

**Cayman Islands
Department of Tourism**
6100 Blue Lagoon Dr. #150
Miami, FL 33126
305-266-2300

**China National
Tourist Office**
333 W. Broadway #201
Glendale, CA 91204
818-545-7505

**China National
Tourist Office**
350 5th Ave. #6413
New York, NY 10118
212-760-9700

**Colombian
Consulate**
1825 Connecticut
Ave., NW
Washington, DC 20009
202-332-7476

**Colombian
Consulate**
500 N. Michigan Ave.
#2040
Chicago, IL 60611
312-923-9434

**Costa Rican
Tourist Board**
800-343-6332

Cyprus Tourist Office
13 East 40th St.
New York, NY 10016
212-683-5280

Czech Center
1109 Madison Ave.
New York, NY 10028
212-288-0830

Denmark Tourist Board
655 3rd Ave.
New York, NY 10017
212-949-2333

**Egyptian Tourist
Authority**
630 Fifth Ave. #1706
New York, NY 10111
212-332-2570

Finland
(see Scandanavia)

**French Government
Tourist Office**
444 Madison Ave.,
16th floor
New York, NY 10022
212-838-7800

**French Government
Tourist Office**
676 N. Michigan Ave.
#3360
Chicago, IL 60611
900-990-0040
or 312-751-7800

**German National
Tourist Office**
122 East 42nd St.
New York, NY 10068
212-661-7200

**German National
Tourist Office**
11766 Wilshire Blvd. #750
Los Angeles, CA 90025
310-575-9799

**Greek National
Tourist Organization**
645 Fifth Ave.
New York, NY 10022
212-421-5777

**Greek National
Tourist Organization**
611 W. 6th St. #2198
Los Angeles, CA 90017
213-626-6696

**Greek National
Tourist Organization**
168 N. Michigan Ave. #600
Chicago, IL 60601
312-782-1084

**Grenada Department
of Tourism**
820 Second Ave.
New York, NY 10017
800-927-9554

Haiti Tourist Information
65 E. Wacker Place #2200
Chicago, IL 60601
312-346-9107

**Hong Kong
Tourist Association**
590 Fifth Ave.
New York, NY 10036
212-869-5008

**Hong Kong
Tourist Association**
10940 Wilshire
Blvd. #1220
Los Angeles, CA 90024
310-208-4582
or 800-282-HKTA

Hungarian Tourist Board
150 E. 58th St. 33rd floor
New York, NY 10022
212-355-0240

Iceland Tourist Board
655 Third Ave. #1810
New York, NY 10017
212-949-2333 ext.130

India Tourist Office
1270 Avenue of the
Americas, Suite 1808
New York, NY 10020
212-586-4901

Indonesian Tourist Office
3457 Wilshire Blvd.
Los Angeles, CA 90010
213-387-2078

Ireland Tourist Board
345 Park Ave.
New York, NY 10154
212-418-0800
or 800-223-6470

**Israel Government
Tourist Office**
800 Second Ave. 16th floor
New York, NY 10017
800-596-1199

**Israel Government
Tourist Office**
5 S. Wabash
Chicago, IL 60603
312-782-4306

**Italian Government
Travel Office**
500 N. Michigan
Ave. #2240
Chicago, IL 60611
312-644-0996

Italian Tourist Office
630 Fifth Ave.
New York, NY 10020
212-245-4822

**Italian Government
Tourist Board**
12400 Wilshire Blvd.
Los Angeles, CA 90025
310-820-0098

Jamaican Tourist Board
801 Second Ave.
New York, NY 10017
212-856-9727
or 800-233-4582

**Japan National
Tourist Office**
360 Post St. #601
San Francisco, CA 94108
415-989-7140

**Japan National
Tourist Organization**
1 Rockefeller Plaza #1250
New York, NY 10020
212-757-5640

Jordan Embassy
202-966-2664 Ext. 116

Kenya Tourist Office
424 Madison Ave. #1401
New York, NY 10017
212-486-1300

Kenya Tourist Office
9150 Wilshire Blvd. #160
Beverly Hills, CA 90212
310-274-6635

**Korean National
Tourism Organization**
205 N. Michigan Ave.
#2212
Chicago, IL 60601
312-819-2560

**Korean National
Tourism Office**
2 Executive Dr. #750
Ft. Lee, NJ 07024
201-585-0909

**Korean National
Tourist Office**
3435 Wilshire Blvd. #1110
Los Angeles, CA 90010
213-382-3435

**Luxembourg National
Tourist Office**
17 Beekman Place
New York, NY 10017
212-935-8888

**Malaysian
Tourist Center**
818 West 7th St.
Los Angeles, CA 90017
213-689-9702

**Mexican Government
Tourism Office**
5075 Westheimer #975W
Houston, TX 77056
713-629-1611

**Mexican Government
Tourism Office**
2333 Ponce de Leon Blvd.
#710
Miami, FL 33134
305-443-9160

**Mexican Government
Tourism Office**
70 E. Lake St. #1413
Chicago, IL 60601
312-606-9015

**Mexican Government
Tourism Office**
405 Park Ave. #1402
New York, NY 10022
212-755-7261

Mexican Tourist Office
10100 Santa Monica Blvd.
Los Angeles, CA 90067
310-203-8191
or 800-44-MEXICO

Monaco Government
Tourist Office
565 5th Ave.
New York, NY 10017
800-753-9696

Morocco National
Tourist Office
20 East 46th St.
New York, NY 10017
212-557-2520

Nepal Tourist
Information
820 2nd Ave. #202
New York, NY 10017
212-370-4188

Netherlands
Board of Tourism
225 N. Michigan Ave. #326
Chicago, IL 60601
312-819-1500
or 888-GO HOLLAND

Netherlands Board
of Tourism
355 Lexington Ave.
New York, NY 10017
800-95-DUTCH

Netherlands Board
of Tourism
9841 Airport Blvd.
Los Angeles, CA 90045
310-348-9339

New Zealand
Tourist Office
501 Santa Monica Blvd.
Santa Monica, CA 90401
310-395-7480
or 800-388-5494

Norway Scandinavia
Tourist Offices
655 Third Ave.
New York, NY 10017
212-949-2333

Peru Consulate General
215 Lexington Ave.,
21st floor
New York, NY 10016
212-481-7410

Peruvian Embassy
Cultural Dept.
1700 Massachusetts Ave.
Washington, DC 20036
202-833-9860

Philippine Tourism Office
Phillipine Center
556 5th Ave.
New York, NY 10036
212-575-7915

Polish National Tourist
Office
275 Madison Ave. #1711
New York, NY 10016
212-338-9412

Portuguese Tourism Office
590 Fifth Ave.
New York, NY 10036
212-354-4403

Puerto Rican Tourism Office
575 5th Ave.
New York, NY 10017
800-223-6530

Russian Tourist Office
800 3rd Ave. #3101
New York, NY 10022
212-758-1162

Scandanavian Tourist Board
655 3rd Ave., 18th floor
New York, NY 10017
212-949-2333

Singapore Tourist Board
590 Fifth Ave.
New York, NY 10036
212-302-4861

Singapore Tourist Promotion Board
8484 Wilshire Blvd. #510
Beverly Hills, CA 90211
213-852-1901

Singapore Tourist Promotion Board
180 N. Stetson Ave. #1450
Chicago, IL 60601-6710
312-938-1888

South African Tourism Board
747 Third Ave.
New York, NY 10017
212-838-8841
or 800-822-5368

South African Tourism Board
9841 Airport Blvd. #1524
Los Angeles, CA 90045
310-641-8444
or 800-782-9772

Spanish National Tourism Office
666 5th Ave., 35th floor
New York, NY 10103
212-265-8822

Spanish Tourist Office
845 N. Michigan Ave. #915E
Chicago, IL 60601
312-642-1992
or 800-OKSPAIN

Spanish Tourist Office
8383 Wilshire Blvd. #960
Beverly Hills, CA 90211
213-658-7188

Sri Lankan Tourist Board
2148 Wyoming Ave.
Washington, DC 20008
202-483-4025

Swedish Tourist Board
655 Third Ave.
New York, NY 10017
212-949-2333

**Swiss National
Tourist Office**
608 Fifth Ave.
New York, NY 10020
212-757-5944

**Swiss National
Tourist Office**
150 N. Michigan Ave.
#2930
Chicago, IL 60601
312-332-9900

**Swiss National
Tourist Office**
222 N. Sepulveda Blvd.
El Segunda, CA 90245
310-640-8900

**Taiwan Visitors
Association**
One World Trade Center
New York, NY 10048
212-466-0691

**Thailand Tourism
Authority**
3440 Wilshire Blvd.
Los Angeles, CA 90010
213-382-2353

**Thailand Tourism
Authority**
303 E. Wacker Dr. #400
Chicago, IL 60601
312-819-3990

**Thailand Tourism
Authority**
5 World Trade Center
#3443
New York, NY 10048
212-432-0433

**Tunisian
Tourist Office**
1515 Massachusetts Ave.,
NW
Washington, DC 20005
202-862-1850

**Turkish
Tourism Office**
821 United Nations Plaza
New York, NY 10017
212-687-2194

**Turkish
Tourist Office**
1717 Massachusetts Ave.,
NW #306
Washington, DC 20036
202-429-9844

**Venezuelan
Tourism Association**
P.O. Box 3010
Sausalito, CA 94966
415-331-0100

**Zimbabwe
Tourist Office**
1270 Ave. of the Americas
#2315
New York, NY 10020
212-332-1090

Newsletters On Solo Travel

Some of these newsletters are written for women, though almost all the information they contain is of equal interest to men, so I encourage my male readers to subscribe anyway.

Connecting is published every other month, six times a year. Send a check or money order for $25 for a one year subscription ($30 Canadian) or $5 for a sample copy to PO Box 29088, 1996 W. Broadway, Vancouver, BC, Canada V6J 5C2 or call 800-557-1757. *Connecting* is 16 pages of first-hand travel accounts as well as tips on avoiding high single-room supplement charges. A subscription includes a copy of the *Single-Friendly Travel Directory* offering hundreds of contacts.

Journeywoman Online Magazine is free and informative. Visit this award-winning site at http://www.journeywoman.com where travel stories and travel tips await you. Subscribe to the free e-mail newsletter.

Maiden Voyages, a quarterly magazine, offers fascinating articles and practical information clearly aimed at the woman traveler. Subscriptions are $16. Call 800-528-8425. Extensive tour information may be found at their Web site, http://www.maiden-voyages.com.

Smart Woman Traveler, a 12-page newsletter, is published 11 times a year. Its aim is to expand the comfort zone of female travelers. Each issue features information on a particular destination in addition to a wealth of other practical information, much of it gleaned from other publications. Subscriptions may be ordered by calling 800-250-8428.

Solo Dining Savvy, the 8-page newsletter devoted to "taking the bite out of eating alone" is published every other month, six times a year. Filled with strategies and tips on how to increase your comfort and options as a solo diner, it also showcases notable solo-friendly restaurants across the USA and beyond. Subscriptions are $29 per year, a sample copy is $4.50. To order call 800-299-1079.

The Single Traveler is published six times a year. Subscription price for the eight page newsletter is $29 per year. Send a check or money order to PO Box 682, Ross, CA 94957. This informative newsletter, packed with travel tips and articles, advocates better treatment of solo travelers by the travel industry.

Travel Companion Exchange is a singles "personals ads" travel service. Obviously I advocate solo travel, but, if having a companion is all that's going to get you out of the house that first time, you might try this service. Participants range from 28 to 80+ in age, with most on the "mature" side of 50. While I'm hardly in the market for a travel companion, I subscribe to this newsletter for the informative articles and travel tips which fill half of the 44 pages. Call 800-392-1256 to subscribe to this bi-monthly newsletter, or get a sample issue for $6.

Books

A Journey of One's Own, Uncommon Advice for the Independent Woman Traveler, By Thalia Zepatos. Revised 1996 by The Eighth Mountain Press. $16.95

Practical advice for women with accent on extended travel on a very low budget through developing countries. This book has lots of insight into "off the beaten path" travel.

Traveling Solo: Advice and Ideas for More Than 250 Great Vacations, by Eleanor Berman. Published 1997 by The Globe Pequot Press. $16.95

Traveler's Tales, A Woman's World, by Marybeth Bond.
Published 1995 by Traveler's Tales. $17.95
   Compiled travel stories of women who write about their
journeys through Thailand, Mexico, France, Spain and many
more countries.

Index